C000301783

# *Body Language:*

## *The Most Comprehensive Guide on Reading Other People's Behavior. Learn Persuasion and Negotiation Through Powerful Technique of Body Language!*

2

# Table of Contents

# Introduction

All living creatures do it. Communication through body language is something built into our very existence.

You may not know it but subconsciously you are already communicating your feelings, your thoughts, and your emotions through body movements that may seem normal to you. And this goes the other way around, too.

People you regularly interact with are constantly talking to you or someone else without uttering a single word. It can be as obvious as a wink or as subtle as crossed arms.

These actions, conscious or otherwise, can be telltale signs of a person's intent. It's called body language and learning how to read or express yourself through it can help you read someone's personality better or communicate your thoughts more clearly.

But reading and expressing through body language can be tricky without a proper guide. And this is what this book is all about.

With this book, you'll learn all the simplicities and complexities of the human body language. You'll be able to interpret and understand non-verbal cues that may be important to building lasting relationships with other people.

# Chapter 1 - A History of Body Language

Humans have been using body language before written history and even dates back before we invented language. Since we didn't have a way to communicate verbally, our early ancestors had to communicate with each other non-verbally through body signals.

There are signals that are universal to all humans. Let's take smiling, for example. Everyone understands that the action of smiling signifies happiness or satisfaction. It may also express that you don't mean harm to the other party.

Crying, on the other hand, is considered a signal for pain or sadness.

But why are these facial expressions universal and transcends culture and race? Is there are a way for people to understand each other better through body language?

Although there clearly are differences in body language signals between cultures, there are also many which are similar. People may have various racial differences as shown by the color of our skin or even body size and shape but still, we express a lot of body language signals similarly.

So why are all people the same in some aspects when it comes to body language? Research carried out and significant breakthroughs in the last decades may hold the answer.

Body Language Through History

A chimp-like population numbering about 100,000 lived in equatorial Africa around five million years ago. During that time, the African forests were already shrinking in size and the climate was hot and dry. Food gathered by foraging through the canopy was not sufficient anymore so to increase their survival chances, they had to adapt.

The first walking apes existed around 4.4 million years ago according to fossil evidence. They are called Australopithecines and with the ability to walk, they were able to cover longer distances and look for more variety of food. Although this was an evolutionary advantage over other animals, it also made the living environment more complex.

These early human beings were strongly social and to manage the new challenges, the Australopithecines worked in groups. And in order to do that, social interactions needed to be parsed, analyze who are friends and who are foes, and be able to decide which ones should belong to the group and which ones shouldn't. Their mental processing power needed to be upgraded to accommodate this new demand so they adapted by developing bigger brains.

This mental load is the reason why early humans that existed around 2.5 million years ago had brains that are twenty to thirty percent bigger than their predecessors. This means that those who didn't evolve bigger brains were left out and gradually replaced. This period saw the birth of the Homo habilis.

The increase in brain size, however, required more energy which meant the Homo habilis needed to eat more. To meet this requirement, they learned how to eat meat and make tools to use for hunting. Part of their socialization activities included checking each other's fur. Group sizes also became smaller at only around 50 members per group.

The evolution of the human brain continued and its size increased steadily to around 800cc and several major changes took place around 1.7 million years ago. The bigger brain size required better thermal regulation so our early ancestors lost fur and hair, and developed sweat glands to adapt to the change.

Since they had no fur, their skin darkened to protect itself from harmful UV radiation. This led to the appearance of the Homo ergaster and the shift to male-female bonding.

Homo ergaster also lived in groups composed of around 50 members. All communications among members were done using body language. They haven't evolved spoken language yet.

Around a million years ago, the Homo erectus emerged and it was a historic milestone because humans started to spread out of Africa. It was also marked by a much stronger male-female bonding.

Around half a million years ago, Homo Heidelbergensis migrated to Europe and evolved into Neanderthals after a hundred thousand years. These early humans had bigger brains than modern humans and also more muscular.

By around 200,000 years ago, early humans had brains reaching 1400cc which is the same as today's human brain. This led to the emergence of our ancestors, the Homo sapiens.

After several major environmental changes marked with warming and cooling periods, Homo sapiens evolved to modern humans which are behaviorally evolved. That was 50,000 years ago and it's the period when early languages were born.

The development of language presented some critical problems and one of which is reliability. Let's take for example a primate making a sound and using it as a signal. How can the other primates understand and trust this signal? What if it just faked?

Remember that these primates had no sense of morality so they will fake signals for their own benefit. That's why humans developed signals that are difficult to fake through emotionally expressive actions.

To keep from being deceived by fake verbal signals, they needed to be ignored which unfortunately blocks verbal language development. So how did we develop languages?

Communication without the danger of deception required a morally-regulated society. This means that rituals, words, and languages co-evolved together.

Early society relied on a person's adherence to rituals and beliefs in order to check for honesty. This led to the birth of religion.

By then, humans can already communicate with each other via body language and verbal signals.

# Chapter 2 – The Scientific Field of Nonverbal Communication

The greatest human discovery of all time, arguably, is all of us are descendants of a small group of early humans that lived around 50,000 years ago. This fact explains why we are so much alike and why can communicate through body language and express our feelings similarly even though we come from different nationalities and cultures.

This also led to the development of a scientific field dedicated to the study of body language which tried to decode non-verbal cues and signals that people communicate through gestures, facial expressions, postures, and eye movements. Interpreting these actions together with verbal communications helps us understand people better.

The field of body language exists to help us 'read' a person beyond what is being said and even determine if that person is lying. Just as language development is linked to trust and deception concepts, so is the body language field of study.

Body language is all about understanding other people better especially those which are not verbalizing their thoughts and emotions. It can also be about learning how you can hide or cover your attitudes and emotions by faking body language to reach your objectives when you interact with people.

The field of non-verbal communication or body language is divided into different disciplines.

Kinesics

Kinesics is all about interpreting facial expressions and body language or any non-verbal behavior in general. The actions can involve some parts or the whole body.

Ray Birdwhistell coined the term Kinesics in 1952. Birdwhistell was an anthropologist who studied how people communicate with others through non-verbal signals.

He shot films involving people in different social situations and analyzed them to point out specific behavioral patterns. Birdwhistell believed that like spoken language, human body movements had specific meanings that can be interpreted.

Like phoneme in the field of spoken language which represented abstract speed sound used in constructing words, he termed 'kineme' which is a basic movement group used in body language. In his study, Birdwhistell also stated that kinemes should be analyzed in clusters in order to come up with meaningful and valid conclusions.

14

Oculesics

Oculesics deals with the role of the eyes in communication. Eye activities during a conversation such as looking, blinking, and staring are considered important nonverbal signals.

When a person is presented with something that he or she likes, it has been found out that the pupils dilate and the blinking rate increases. When looking at another person the eyes on their own can show a range of emotions such attraction, interest, or even hostility.

Gazing can also provide clues if the other person is lying. When a person makes steady eye contact, it implies that the person is trustworthy and telling the truth. Lack of eye to contact, in contrast, is generally seen as a sign of deception or lying.

Proxemics

Proxemics is a scientific field studying personal space. Edward T. Hall, a cultural anthropologist coined this term in 1963.

Hall's theory on proxemics is separated into two categories – territory and personal space. Territory is about a person's claim on a piece of space and how that person defends it against other people. Personal space, on the other hand, is about how people feel and treat the immediate space around them.

The proxemics field is not limited to studying personal space in humans but has also been used in animals with regards to their behavior surrounding territory and personal space.

Haptics

Haptics is the study of communication through touch and is carried out on both animals and humans. For humans, haptics includes hugging, handshakes, holding hands, kissing, shoulder pat, and even high-fives

Touching is considered to be one of the most fundamental medium of non-verbal communications and is developed as early as the fetal stage. Touch is used for getting information in an environment by sensing surfaces. It's also a vital part of physical intimacy.

Touch gesture interpretation is highly dependent on cultural background, social context, the way the action takes place, and the relationship between the people involved. Different cultures treat touching differently and the levels of touching may also vary.

Certain signals are practiced in some cultures but other cultures may not be able to interpret it or even know how to do it. Like high-fiving, for example.

Vocalics

Humans communicate verbally not just by using the actual language. There are factors to consider such as the vocal pitch, inflection, loudness, and tone. This field of nonverbal communications is called vocalics or paralinguistics.

Let's consider a simple sentence and how the tone of the delivery can have a powerful effect on its meaning. When the sentence is spoken using a strong tone, this is usually interpreted by listeners as a sign of enthusiasm and approval. The same sentence when spoken using a hesitant tone might imply lack of interest of disapproval.

There are a lot of ways that a simple change of the tone of voice can make a sentence mean differently. When someone asks you how you are the immediate answer is "I'm fine" but how you deliver that simple sentence can actually reveal what you are truly feeling that day. When you say it using a cold tone, it can indicate that you're not feeling good and don't want to discuss further. If you use a happy and bright tone, it reveals that you are really feeling good. When delivered with a downcast and somber tone, it also says that you are feeling the opposite and you need someone to talk to about it.

## Animal Behavior

Body language study is also related to animal behavior study which is called ethology. Charles Darwin is considered to be the first modern ethologist and his book, 'The Expression of the Emotions in Man and Animals' is the influence and inspiration of many modern researchers in this field.

Other researches like Julian Huxley expanded the study by observing natural or instinctive behavior in certain species when presented with specific circumstances. Most non-verbal signals are made instinctively so this study explains why humans and other members of the animal kingdom share similar behavior when presented with certain stimuli. The study also provides clues on behavioral conditioning, instinct, psychology, and cognition.

All primates are able to communicate with others using facial expressions. Interestingly, humans and apes use actions that are directed specifically to another individual that they want to communicate with. For example, a chimp that is asking for food stretches his open hand which is considered a begging gesture.

In a study made by Frans de Waal and Amy Pollick, gestures might differ between groups as shown by their observation on chimps and bonobos. There is a significant gesture culture in each group and that bonobos were much more effective communicators using gestures. Bonobos are the only species able to combine both vocal/facial signals and gestures making them multimodal communicators.

De Waal and Pollick suggested that human language evolution must have begun with some sort of gestures vocabulary because specific emotions are disconnected from gestures which makes them easier to control. With facial expressions, you may be able to get a lot of clues about another person's emotional state. Gesture, on the other hand, are easier to use in a deceptive way. Therefore, language must have evolved from gestures.

Artifacts

Images and objects are a couple of tools that can also be used for nonverbal communication. For example, you usually choose an avatar which represents your identity in an online community. This avatar is also often a symbol of who you are in person or the things that you like, or at least who you want other people to see in your personality.

We all spend a significant amount of our time developing a certain personal character as we surround ourselves with objects and images that tell other people about things that are of importance to us. If you want other people to see you as a health buff, you work out to get a good physique and wear clothes that will emphasize those hard-earner muscles or curves.

One example that can be used as a source of information regarding a person is the uniform. When we see someone wearing a fatigue, we immediately think of that person as a soldier. Doctors wear white lab coats and police officers wear uniforms with badges. We can instantly tell what people do for a living by looking at the uniforms they're wearing.

Appearance

A person's choice of hairstyle, clothing, color and other factors related to his appearance can also be considered a type of nonverbal communication. Various researches have shown that colors can affect mood and emotions. Your appearance can also influence interpretations, judgements, and physiological reactions.

Admittedly, all of us make instant judgments based solely on the other person's appearance. First impressions last and that's the reason why it's recommended that you dress appropriately for a job interview because part of how your personality will be evaluated includes how nice you dress up for such an occasion.

There are also studies proving that appearance plays an important role in how you are perceived by other persons. It can even influence how much you get paid. In a study in 1996, attorneys who were considered more attractive compared to their peers earned almost 15 percent more than those considered less attractive.

Culture is a major influence on how people judge appearances. While being thin or slim is generally considered as attractive in Western cultures, some cultures in Africa interpret full-figured people as healthier, wealthier, and belong to a higher social status.

In the next three chapters, we'll dig deeper into three fields that are most closely studied in the science of body language – kinesics, oculesics, and proxemics.

# Chapter 3 – Kinesics

Kinesis means 'movement' and this is where the word kinesics was derived from. Kinesics is the study of face, body, arm, and hand movements. In this chapter we will discuss the use of facial expressions, posture and head movements, and gestures.

Facial Expressions

The face is the most expressive part of the human body. A photo, for example, is able to capture or freeze a certain expression and preserve it for later viewing. Even though a photograph was taken a long time ago, you can still interpret much of the meaning when there is a human face showing a particular emotion. Basic facial expressions are also recognized by most cultures around the world even those located in isolated countries.

A lot of research had been done on the universality of the most common expressions particularly happiness, fear, sadness, anger, disgust, and surprise. The first four in the list were found out to be the most recognizable by all cultures across the globe. However, what causes these expressions to show and which social and cultural norms influence their display seems to be culturally diverse.

Let's take babies, for example. Babies are able to show these expressions at a very young age. Their reactions are also considered purely out of instinct, which make them real. That's why playing peek-a-boo with a baby is so entertaining because you can see the natural expressions of surprise and joy from their faces. As people grow older, we learn more about social norms by following rules on the display of these emotions. We also learn how to control these expressions as suggested by our culture.

A smile is a powerful nonverbal signal and also an immediate indicator of a behavior. Facial expressions are generally thought as innate and some of them are even universally recognizable, but they may not always be connected to internal, biological, or emotional stimuli. Sometimes these expressions are made to serve a purpose that is more social in nature.

Usually we smile to other people as a requirement of the social or cultural norms, but it may not really be a reflection of what we are really feeling inside. However, studies show that these 'typical' smiles can be distinguished from genuine ones. It is said that a real smile involves not only the mouth but also the eyes. This type of smile is hard to fake because the muscles involved in this genuine gesture can't be controlled voluntarily. When these muscles spontaneously contract, they move the skin around the nose, eyes, and cheeks and you get a real smile that looks very different from a social or fake smile. This is the reason why good photographers engage their subjects in cheesy joking or use props for children in order to get a real smile from them when taking pictures.

Facial expressions can also set the emotional tone of a speech. If you want the tone to be positive, you can start by looking at your audience and smiling to communicate confidence, openness, and friendliness. During the speech, you can express different emotions using various facial expressions which you can use to imply personality traits and show competence and credibility. Through facial expressions, a speaker can communicate that he is excited, tired, confused, angry, sad, frustrated, smug, confident, bored, or shy. Showing an animated slack face may indicate that you are bored with the speech even though you are not. So you need to ensure your facial expressions during the speech are sending out the correct personality trait, mood, or emotion that you think the audience views favorably and help you get the results you wanted. The facial expressions you exhibit should also be aligned with the speech content. When discussing a topic that is humorous or light-hearted, you can enhance the message with slightly raised eyebrows, bright eyes, and a smile. When the subject is somber or serious, you can emphasize the speech with a slight nod of the head, a tighter mouth, or a furrowed brow. When the verbal part of the speech is

24

inconsistent with the facial expressions, the audience can get confused on the real intention and your credibility and honesty can be questioned.

Posture and Head Movements

Posture and head movements can be grouped together because these two are often used in acknowledging other persons and communicating attentiveness and interest. When it comes to head movements, for example, the head nod is an acknowledgement sign that is displayed universally especially in cultures where a formal greeting is not anymore done with a bow. Thus, the head nod serves as a summarized bow.

To signify disagreement, the universal body signal is the repeated movement of the head from left to right. This nonverbal cue begins in infancy even before a baby acquires the ability to understand its meaning. A baby might shake the head side to side when rejecting the mother's breast which they later act out in instinct when rejecting attempts of spoon feeding. The nonverbal signal of disagreement is, therefore, based on a biological movement.

The positioning of the head can also signify different behaviors. When a person's head is up, it often indicates either a neutral or engaged attitude. A tilted head imply interest and is also a gesture of submission because it exposes the neck which makes other people feel more trusting of the person. If the head is down, it's often an indication of a negative or even an aggressive attitude.

Human postures are grouped into four general categories – sitting, standing, lying down, and squatting. Each of these postures contain many variations and when these are mixed with certain nonverbal cues or other gestures, they express a lot of different meanings. We converse mostly sitting down or standing up. One common standing posture shown by people is putting the hands on the hips to look bigger and imply assertiveness. With the elbows pointed out, this may mean that no one can get past us. This can also be a sign of dominance or show readiness for action. When sitting, a leaned back posture may show indifference or informality. Straddling the chair can be interpreted as dominance or in certain situations show insecurity because it looks like the person is protecting a vulnerable body part. Leaning forward shows attentiveness and interest.

Gestures

Gestures are categorized into three types – illustrators, emblems, and adaptors. The most common type is illustrators because they are used to 'illustrate' the accompanying verbal message. For example, to indicate the shape or size of an object, you use hand gestures in a conversation. Illustrators are often used subconsciously, and they typically don't have meaning when used on their own.

These gestures are mostly involuntary and naturally flows as we speak. It can also vary in frequency and intensity depending on the context of the conversation. We do illustrator gestures automatically although they are not explicitly taught to us. Most people also use illustrators when talking to someone over the phone even though they can't be seen doing the movements.

Emblems, unlike illustrators which typically don't have context on their own, are gestures which meanings have been agreed on. These are different from the standard sign language used by people who are hearing-impaired when communicating or the American Sign Language (ASL). Emblems are not part of the formal sign systems such as the ASL.

The raised middle finger, the sign for 'OK' with the thumb and index finger forming a circle while the rest of the fingers are sticking up, and the hitchhiker's thumb are examples of emblems. Each one of these have meanings that have been agreed on with a culture. Emblems can be stationary or moving. When you circle your index finger around the side of the head, it's an agreed sign for the word 'crazy' and pumping your arm up and down with your fist closed means 'hurry up!'.

The origin of a word can be traced back through its etymology. Some nonverbal signals, particularly emblems, also have history. When you hold your index and middle fingers up forming a 'V' shape, it's an insult to British people. The gesture dates back to a period when the bow and arrow was the primary war weapon. When an archer is captured, the enemy would cut these two fingers off as an insult because it means the archer can no longer use a bow and arrow. Holding up these two fingers is a form of mockery showing that they still have their archer fingers intact.

Adaptors refer to touching movements and behaviors indicating internal states and are typically linked to anxiety or arousal. These types of gestures can be directed toward the self, an object, or other persons. Adaptors are generally a result of anxiety, uneasiness, or a sense of losing control of a situation. Most people subconsciously shake their legs, click pens, or show other adaptor gestures during meetings, classes, or while waiting. This is somewhat a way to burn the excess energy.

Have you ever watched a video of yourself speaking in public? Did you notice nonverbal adaptors you didn't know you used? During public speeches, most people use object or self-focused adaptors. Examples of common self-adaptors are coughing or throat-clearing actions. Some are more inclined to object adaptors like fiddling with the mic or the wire while speaking. Others may play with the note cards, whiteboard markers, or coins in their pockets. Boredom can also trigger adaptors such as peeling off labels from a beer bottle or fiddling with the drinking straw. Adaptors are actually more commonly found in social rather than public speaking scenarios mainly because of the distance between the speaker and the audience.

# Chapter 4 – Oculesics

Oculesics is the study of the eye's role in body language. It is derived from oculus, a Latin word which means 'eye'. People communicate using eye behavior, particularly eye contact.

During a conversation, the eyes and faces are often the main focus. The eyes, along with the ears, also receive most of the information. It's said that the eyes are the window to one's soul. This saying is actually accurate because the eyes can express a lot of emotions or show nonverbal signals even though a person is trying to hide them.

Some eye behaviors have also been tied to emotional states or personality traits as you often hear them in phrases such as 'bedroom eyes', 'evil eyes', and 'hungry eyes'. To understand oculesics better, here are the functions and characteristics of pupil dilation and eye contact.

Eye contact is a powerful body signal and is used in establishing personal connections, conveying information, or monitoring and regulating interactions. During a conversation we often express our desire to speak using eye contact or use it to cue other people to speak up.

Regulating Interactions

You may have been in that common awkward situation wherein the teacher is asking a question and no one is raising a hand to answer. He or she then looks directly at you as if saying 'what do you think?' without even speaking a word. The teacher is actually using eye contact to cue the students to speak up. So those who don't know the answer avoids eye contact by looking elsewhere around the room.

As a person changes from being a speaker to being a listener, eye contact also changes. In a classroom scenario, the teacher might avoid eye contact while discussing the lesson and only make them when he's waiting for a response from the class. He or she also often use eye contact to conclude the discussion as a cue that he or she is finishing up. A student, on the other hand, maintains eye contact with the teacher during the lesson to show attentiveness and also gather information.

Monitoring Interactions

Eye contact can also be used in getting feedback or other body signals and sending back information. Through the eyes, we gather visual information from other people such as their eye behaviors, gestures, postures, and movements. Through visual observation, a speaker can determine if his audience is bored, confused, or engaged. He or she can then make the necessary adjustments to his message or delivery.

We also use our eyes to send information to other people. When we are in deep thought, we tend to look away from other people which is a way of signaling them not to bother us. When we make eye contact, we are implying interest and attention to the speaker or the discussion. This makes the eyes important tools in listening.

Engaging or Disengaging

Using eye contact we can convey either interest or disinterest. When we look attentively and make longer eye contact with someone, it tells them that you are engaged with the discussion and want the conversation to continue. When you look away, it's a sign that you want to disengage and go away.

In public settings such as gyms or airports where it's common for people to make small talk with strangers, you can signal that you don't want to be disturbed by avoiding eye contact with other people. You can also wear sunglasses to the same effect. But when you want to speak to someone you are attracted to, you try to establish eye contact with him or her with a plan to start a conversation.

Flirting or Intimidating

The duration of the eye contact also carries a meaning. This meaning, however, is often dictated by social or cultural norms, the environment or setting, and your relationship between the two people. In certain situations, staring can be taken as an act of intimidation, such as after a verbal argument. In more intimate scenarios, a long stare is an effective nonverbal cue for flirting with someone especially if both parties know each other personally.

Pupil Dilation

The dilation of the pupils is also studied in the field of oculesics although it doesn't get as much attention as eye contact or eye movement. Pupil dilation is the contraction or expansion of the pupils of the eyes and is a biometric measurement form. This action is involuntary which means you can't consciously control it making it a reliable source of nonverbal cues.

When light is insufficient for us to see clearly, the eyes compensate by dilating or enlarging the pupil to let in more light. When there is enough or too much light, the pupils contract or become smaller. Pupil dilation can also be affected by sexual attraction, pain, stress or anxiety, general arousal, and information processing.

Researchers measure and study pupil dilation for a variety of reasons. Advertisers use it to determine consumer preferences because when a person is attracted to the product, the pupils dilate.

Although we may not be consciously interpreting pupil dilation while we talk to other people, we do so subconsciously, and this has an effect on the conversation.

# Chapter 5 – Proxemics

Proxemics is the field body language that explains how distance and space affect communication. Relationships, communication, and space are closely related as seen in the many ways space is a factor in common metaphors. When you are attracted or content with someone, you say you are 'close' to that person. When this connection is lost, you often say the person appears 'distant'. Space, therefore, has a big influence on how we behave and communicate with each other.

In a small space occupied by many people, personal space bubbles are more likely to be breached. If this scenario is known beforehand, such as a train during rush hour or a crowded concert, managing the space issue requires different communication adjustments. When personal space is breached unexpectedly, it can lead to stressed situations especially if the violation of personal space was made intentionally and without permission which means crowding didn't force that violator into your space.

Research shows that crowding can also lead to delinquent or criminal behavior referred to as 'mob mentality'. In their minds, if everyone is doing it, it must be right.

## Proxemic Distances

People have different definitions of 'personal space'. These definitions can be contextual and may depend on the relationship and the situation. Although a personal space bubble is invisible, people recognize it because of cultural and social upbringing. Scholars categorized four proxemics zones for US Americans namely, intimate, personal, social, and public distances. These zones take up more space in the front or the person's line of sight and is smaller on the sides and back.

## Intimate Zone

The intimate zone is defined at around 1.5 feet from the body. This zone is reserved only to family, closest friends, and intimate or romantic partners. When other people are inside this space, it's impossible to ignore them even if we pretend to. While a breach of the intimate zone is comforting in some situations, it can be frightening or at least annoying to others.

People need regular verbal and physical human contact because touch is an important part of our relationship with others. For a physical touch to happen, people need to enter our own intimate zone. When words fail to deliver, feeling someone's physical presence and being close to them is quite comforting.

This degree of closeness is sometimes displayed in public depending on the social and cultural norms. Some people can feel uncomfortable when seeing displays of intimacy while some can comfortably engage in it or watch others do it.

Personal Zone

Personal zone extends around 1.5 to 4 feet from our physical body. This space is reserved for close acquaintance, friends, and other significant persons. Most conversations occur in this personal space and this is what people refer to as their personal space bubble. Even though the personal space is pretty close to the body of other person, verbal communication can be used to imply that presence in this space is friendly in nature but not intimate.

The personal zone is further divided into two sub-zones. The outer personal space extends 2.5 to 4 feet and is the zone where private conversations may take place even though both parties are not really that close. Communication that is relatively intimate is allowed in this zone such as professional conversations. The inner personal space extends 1.5 to 2.5 feet and is reserved for communicating with people having interpersonal relationships with us or those we want to get to know better. Touching while talking is normally allowed in this zone to facilitate feelings of closeness and self-disclosure.

Social Zone

The social zone extends 4 to 12 feet away from the body is where casual or professional communication takes place but not public or intimate. In most professional conversations, this zone is more preferred. When you 'keep someone at an arm's length', it means you let that person in your personal space. When two people extend both their arms with the tips of their fingers touching, they'll be standing about 4 feet from each other making the social space both personal and professional.

Student's in a class, for example, are often positioned within the social zone of the teacher. This proximity allows better interaction while still avoiding too much intimacy.

Public Zone

This space extends 12 feet or more from the body making it the least personal out of the four zones. This space is typically used during formal speeches made in auditoriums. Although the speaker reaches out to the audience, they're also isolated. This distance can be taken as a sign of authority or power and applies to celebrities and politicians. You are not expected or obligated to interact or acknowledge people within your public zone. Having personal conversations is difficult at this distance and you have to talk louder because it lacks the physical closeness required to establish rapport and initiate emotional closeness.

# Chapter 6 – Body Language Myths You Should Know About

Body language plays a big part in communication so learning how to read and express yourself through nonverbal cues is a skill you should develop. But when body language is mentioned, audiences are divided into skeptics and over-believers. The skeptics doubt the effectiveness of interpreting body language when trying to read what the other person is really thinking about. The over-believers think that nonverbal signals are always reliable.

Here are some body language myths that you should be aware of.

You Can Fake Body Language

Deception will always be a part of man's way of life that's why people are always looking for ways to deceive when needed. Some people may view lying as morally wrong but that's a different issue altogether. But can you fake your body language and how is it useful?

The experts are actually divided on this topic. One group believes that it's not possible to fake body signals. They argue that most facial expressions and other body gestures are produced unconsciously and they're extremely difficult to reproduce naturally and consciously. When a person experiences a particular emotion, he tends to show a lot of nonverbal cues that faking all of them will be impossible. And when that person is just pretending or acting out the emotion without actually feeling it, these signals become so unnatural that it's easy to point the anomaly out and conclude that something is wrong.

At the other side of the fence, a group claims that people can learn how to fake particular signals and you can use it to establish and improve rapport with other people, making them feel more relaxed when they're around you. This group is composed mostly of Neuro-Linguistic Programming or NLP fans. Their methods emphasize the knowledge of reading eye movement and mirroring and some users of their methods claim that they actually work.

Both groups actually have their own valid points. Whichever group you think has the correct way of thinking, remember that it doesn't hurt to try. When you are learning body language, your ultimate goal should be improving the overall quality of your conversations which will then allow you to get the desired results. This is true whether you are reading body language or faking it.

This may sound a tad selfish but let's admit it, it's what everybody wants so denying it is pointless and futile. If you think a certain method is working for you, then use it to your advantage. If you are using a significantly effective eye-contact technique or any particular nonverbal cues that give you positive results, go ahead and get the most out of them.

Some people may see faking body language as a form of deception which is not the right way to view the subject. When you are about to give an important presentation, you plan not only the content of the message but also how you want it delivered to the audience. As you already know, communication is not just pure spoken language. There's a nonverbal part of it that is equally important. That's why when you prepare your script by listing the things you want to say, you also need to practice your actions as you say them. Preparing for the verbal part of the presentation doesn't make it inauthentic, right? The same goes for the nonverbal cues that will help you make the most emphasis and reach out to your audience more. The problem, therefore, lies in the overall delivery. When you say something wrong and off the prepared script, your audience might react negatively. The same goes when your body language does not align with what you're saying or you're not using the appropriate nonverbal cues to emphasize points in your presentation. Showing the wrong facial expressions and gestures at the wrong time is a formula for losing your audience's interest. So, you should be practicing both the verbal and nonverbal aspects of your presentation because these are the keys for delivering a convincing performance.

You Can Spot a Lie Using Body Language

There have been many articles published by experts and non-experts alike claiming that certain body language signals that indicate a person is definitely lying. This trend was most noticeable during the 70s when body language advocates believed that particular nonverbal cues can be used in exposing lying individuals. These 'experts' even claimed that the same techniques can be used in solving criminal cases. You may already know most of these nonverbal signals and gestures. Here are some of them:

- Covering the mouth

- Touching the nose

- High-pitched voice while talking

- Closing the eyes

- Scratching or touching the neck

- Pulling the ear

In 1985, some researchers, which included Paul Ekman, decided it was time to analyze the claims scientifically in order to evaluate the myth. The result of the research showed that when using pure body language as the indicator that someone is lying, there is only a 50/50 chance of hitting it right, which is pretty much random.

In their report, they said that the signals do not directly indicate that a person is lying but they are just indication that that person is stressed. When a person is stressed when answering a question, that doesn't necessarily mean he is lying. It's just another body signal among many others.

This is much more apparent in stressful scenarios such as a crime investigation. When a person is accused of committing the crime, he will be quite stressed as he goes through the experience whether he is guilty or not. He will be showing signs of stress, which is a natural reaction given the situation which, in this case, shouldn't be interpreted as deception. The stress levels can sometimes be so great that the person accused may admit he is guilty just to get away from the stressful ordeal.

In short, detecting signals should only be the start of the lie detection process and should not be used as the only and all-conclusive evidence. Nonverbal cues should only be treated as one of the many clues. For detailed discussion on lie detection using body language, we've got a full chapter dedicated to that.

Culture Defines Body Language

Paul Ekman also got involved in the scientific investigation during his pioneering research in 2003. In the study, pictures of people showing six fundamental facial expressions were shown to 21 people each belonging to different cultures from all over the world. The expressions showed fear, happiness, sadness, anger, disgust, and surprise. It turned out that most of the test subjects were able to recognize the emotions showed.

The study even included an isolated tribe that were still living with ancient tools and traditions and they, too, were able to recognize these facial expressions and the associated emotions. The tribe mentioned was the South Fore people from New Guinea, which were isolated from modern culture, particularly the Western. When they saw the pictures, they immediately associated with the emotions being shown but they had a hard time distinguishing between surprise and fear. What Paul did was take the pictures of people from the tribe showing fear and surprise. He then showed the pictures to Americans and they were able to recognize the right emotions being shown. This research showed that facial expressions, at least the very fundamental ones, are universal and can be mostly recognized by people from any part of the world.

But other nonverbal cues are not universal. Some of the manners and behavior that people exhibit is developed through cultural conditioning. Thus, people from different parts of the worlds can be expressing gestures that may mean differently across various cultures. Learning these gestures and how they are interpreted by different cultures is very critical because mistakes can potentially lead to feeling offended, acting offensively, and discrimination although it was not the original intention.

For example, when a person is avoiding eye contact, this is generally interpreted as a sign of deception or lying. But people from Africa or Latin America have been taught from childhood not to look directly into the eyes of people with authority like the elderly, their bosses, or religious and political leaders. This can be a problem in a scenario wherein a police officer in a western country is questioning a person with the mentioned cultural upbringing. That person will try to avoid looking into the eyes of the police office because that reaction was developed in him since childhood. The police officer, in contrast, might interpret this gesture as a sign that the other person is trying to hide something. For more detailed cultural differences in body language, there is a dedicated discussion of the subject in another chapter.

To Show Power, Put Your Hands at Your Back

Some body language coaches may advice people that putting your hands behind your back is a show of authority or power. Prince Charles adopt the same posture and he is royalty, right? Unfortunately, that may not be the case when you imitate the posture.

In the contrary, most people who are confronted using this particular posture find the other person untrustworthy. This means that putting your hands behind you because you want to impose superiority on another person is a myth, after all.

There's even a negative connotation to this gesture. Generally, the other person might interpret your action of hiding your hands behind your back as a way to hide something from them. When you want to show that you are open to ideas or is not hostile, you should expose your hands particularly your palms. This implies that you have nothing to hide and is a gesture proven to establish trust and rapport.

A Person with Crossed Arms is Being Defensive

In its absolute form, this statement is a myth. You should not be interpreting a single gesture as an indication of the what the other person is feeling or trying to say. Gestures should be read in context and the environment or scenario taken into consideration. These nonverbal cues should be read in clusters rather than interpreted individually.

A person in a cold room sitting in a chair with his arms crossed over his cheat may not be being defensive. He might simply be feeling cold. That's why all body signals should be read with reference to all other gestures and combined with the verbal signals.

The next chapter will dive deeper into the basics of reading nonverbal cues and should provide more knowledge on how to properly interpret body language. A particular behavior or emotion is always shown as a collection of different body signals. Relying on just one won't give you an accurate reading.

# Chapter 7 - How to Understand Nonverbal Cues and its Benefits

Whether you are out with friends or inside the office with workmates, body language says a lot about other people. Studies say that body language comprise more than sixty percent of communication which makes learning how to read or interpret nonverbal signals that other people send a very valuable skill.

Body language can reveal what people are really thinking about and can be interpreted through various signals from their eye behavior and to which direction their feet are pointing. Here are some important tips that can help you understand body language better and understand other people.

Eye Behavior

The eye behavior of the other person can be very revealing. When you communicate with people, observe if they look away or make eye contact with you. Not making direct eye contact can imply disinterest, boredom, and sometimes even deception – particularly when that person looks away and then to the side. A person looking down may be signaling submissiveness or nervousness.

You can also check if the eyes' pupils become dilated which is a sign that the other person is responding favorably to you. When there is an increase in cognitive effort, a person's pupils dilate, and this means that someone is focused on what you are saying.

This dilation process can be quite difficult to spot depending on your proximity from the other person or the color of their eyes, but you should be able to detect it under proper conditions.

The rate at which the person blinks can also mean a lot. When people are stressed or overthinking, the blinking rate increases. Lying or hiding something can also cause rapid blinking and is even more obvious when the person is touching the face particularly in the mouth or nose areas.

When someone glances at something, it may be a sign of desire. For example, a person glancing at the door might be signaling that he or she wants to leave the room. Glancing at another person might mean a desire to talk.

You may be able to tell if a person is lying by the movement of their eyes when talking about something. When that person looks upward and then right, it can indicate a lie while looking up and to the left indicate truth. This is because people look up and right when creating a story through imagination and look to the left when recalling a real memory.

Facial Gestures

Although it can be particularly easy to control facial expression, you can still find some nonverbal cues if you are attentive enough.

Focus on the other person's mouth when interpreting nonverbal signals. A smile is a very effective and powerful gesture which may contain important nonverbal cues. Smiles can be categorized into different types including genuine and fake ones.

When a person smiles genuinely, the whole face is engaged. Fake smiles only engage the mouth. A genuine smile means that person is happy and enjoys the company of the people around him. When someone is faking a smile, it may be to convey approval or pleasure while trying to hide what is truly being felt. Uncertainty or sarcasm is usually expressed with a half-smile which engages only a side of the mouth. You may even see a grimace before the fake smile which may indicate dissatisfaction.

Relaxed mouth and lips can indicate a positive mood and a relaxed attitude. Lips that are pursed tightly may be implying displeasure. When someone is touching the lips or covering the mouth with the fingers, it may indicate that person is lying.

## Proximity

Proximity is how physically close you are to the other person. Notice how someone sits or stands next to you. Sitting or standing close together can indicate rapport between people. If the other person backs or moves away, they may be thinking that the connection is not mutual.

Different cultures might have different views on the accepted proximity during conversations. This will be discussed in detail in another chapter.

## Mirroring

Mirroring means copying the body language of the other person. If the other person is mirroring your behavior (posture, sitting or standing position, gestures, talking speed), it may indicate a desire to establish rapport. To confirm this behavior, change your posture and see if the other person mimics it as well.

## Head Movement

Head movements are also considered critical non-verbal cues. The universally accepted signal for 'yes' is nod while for 'no' it's moving the head sideways. Learning how to notice subtle head movements can give you a clearer insight on another person's thoughts.

The other person might be verbally agreeing to what you are saying but you noticed that he subtly shook his head sideways. It can be tricky to catch this movement, but this is a signal that he doesn't agree with you at all.

The speed of the head movement can also be a source for clues. A slow nod typically indicates that the other person is genuinely interested and wants you to continue talking. A fast nodding action can imply impatience.

When the head is tilted sideways, it can also indicate interest or submissiveness to the idea. But if the head is tilted backwards, this is usually a sign that they don't believe you.

Gestures

Signals made with hands are very obvious which makes them very direct means of communicating non-verbally. When a person points at something without uttering a word, you look in that direction. Signaling small numbers is also a very common gesture. A thumbs up is a common gesture of approval while a thumbs down says otherwise.

Although most of these gestures can be easily interpreted and understood, they may have different meanings across cultures. That's why it's important to get to know the other person's cultural upbringing before using certain gestures since some of these may be considered offensive or obscene.


## Arm Positions and Movements

Besides gestures, the positioning and movement of your hands also gives away nonverbal cues to the person you're talking to. Placing an elbow on top of your desk and supporting your head with one hand can indicate that you are focused and attentive on the discussion. But when you use two hands, it may imply boredom.

When you put your hands behind your back when conversing can be interpreted as anger, deceit, or boredom. When you cross your arms in front, it's an indication of being defensive because you're 'guarding' yourself.

When you put your arms on the hips while standing and talking to another person, it's a signal of taking control or being assertive. In certain situations, some people may see it as aggression.

## Your Feet

Your feet can also be a rich source of nonverbal signals just like your arms. In fact, cues being shown using the feet are more natural and genuine because they often happen intentionally.

A person trying to deceive someone might consciously be able to control hand movements, facial expression, or posture but it's easy to forget that the feet are also sending signals. The feet tend to point towards the direction where the mind wants to go. This is true whether the person is sitting or standing.

If another person's feet are pointing to our, it can be a sign that you are being received favorably and that they want you to continue the conversation. If the feet are pointing away, that person might be thinking of getting away from you or leaving the conversation. They might be showing interest by smiling at you or pretending to be listening, but the feet are saying otherwise.

The positioning of the legs can also give out hints about a person's inner thoughts. Open legs can signify the person is comfortable with the conversation while crossed legs is a cue that they are protecting their privacy.

Postures

You might remember your mother always telling you no to slouch. Slouching is bad for your posture and people tend to perceive you on how you hold your body up. Our posture can also be an expression of how we are feeling.

Body posture shows when you're feeling confident, open, submissive, or fearful. When you stand or sit upright with the head held high and the back straight, you are seen as someone who is alert, active, and confident.

When you hold this same upright posture while listening to another person talking, it implies that you are being attentive, and you're interested in what is being discussed.

When you hold you head low while you sit or stand with the back hunched forward, it's a sign that you lack confidence or that you're sad or lazy. It can also be seen as a lack of interest.

Benefits of Understanding Body Language

People communicate with both verbal and nonverbal signals so knowing how to interpret and read the nonverbal cues is as important as listening to the words being spoken. Here are the benefits of understanding body language.

1.  Better connection with people

    Around 60-90% of communication is done using body language according to different studies. Learning to read body language and expressing yourself better through it can help establish better connections with other people.

Learning body language can expand your communication skills. With it, you can pick up gestures that may reveal more than what the other person is saying and can help you see the clearer picture.

2. Increase Business Prospects

Learning body language is important to entrepreneurs. Accurate recognition of a customer's or partner's body language can help you grow your business. Missing important nonverbal cues can lead to misunderstanding and affect business relationships.

For example, you are doing a sales pitch and you fail to notice the gestures of a prospective client. He or she may already be showing signs of being uninterested or bored. If you know how to notice and read these signals, you can adjust your own body language to synch with theirs and immediately establish rapport.

3. Prevent Conflicts

Since a significant part of human communications is nonverbal, it's particularly important to detect when negative emotions or misunderstandings are beginning to creep up during a conversation. When we're upset or angry, we tend to use a special body language type. We take on a defensive body position and also show our anger through facial expressions and body gestures.

When you are aware of these nonverbal signals, you will be able to accurately interpret anger coming from the other person and to implement measures to keep the situation from escalating. There are numerous negative remarks or even physical conflicts that could be prevented if you have proper body language insights.

4. Improve Personal Presence

Learning about body language is not all about knowing how to interpret other people's nonverbal cues but also understanding yours, as well. What kinds of body language signals do you tend to send out? How does the other person perceive you and your actions? How are they interpreting your posture?

As you learn more about body language, you also become much more aware of the nonverbal signals you are sending.

You soon become conscious of the placement of your arms, how you tilt your head, how you sit or stand up, and other gestures. You also learn about their meanings so you can use them to your advantage.

You can actually study body language even without another person around. Notice that when you're watching a movie you like at home you feel relaxed and loose. But when a character that you don't like enters the scene, you become more tensed and anxious? You may react by crossing your legs and arms as a way of 'nonverbal blocking'. That's body language in action. If you didn't know about this particular gesture, you'll pass it off as just a normal reaction, which it is. But having knowledge of body language gives you the chance to change this behavior.

Another significant advantage of body language in improving personal presence is that you can use it to change how you feel. For example, standing up, holding the head high, and expanding your chest can actually make you feel better when you are down, listless, or depressed. Hold this position for a couple of minutes and you will start feeling more confident and more energetic. When you improve your body language, you'll begin having positive impact not only to other people but also yourself.

5. Open Your World

The latest model of a smartphone you like is out and you really want to get your hands on one. You'll notice that you're seeing them almost everywhere. You'll see more people having it, more advertisements showing it, and even people you know talking about it. Does that mean the product has been sold thousands of times that you start seeing it more and more? Probably not. Your attraction to that smartphone has trained your brain to look for it which explains why you seem to see it much more often.

The same applies to body language. You may not yet be aware of it but there are a lot of other things going on in a conversation besides the exchange of words. In half an hour, a person could be sending more than 800 nonverbal cues. Imagine the wealth of information you could gather if you know how to interpret them.

Knowing how to interpret body language is like seeing the world clearer and more accurately. It's an extra layer of data and information that you can use to communicate better.

# Chapter 8 - Can You Detect a Lie Through Body Language?

Perhaps the main reason why people are interested with body language is that they want to know if they are being deceived. We are so obsessed with learning how to spot liars and maybe even learn how to lie effectively.

We all lie, that's a given fact. We do it even if it's socially unaccepted or morally wrong. Some people have even made the action of lying a habit and have become such good liars that they believe their own lies.

You come home to your wife and while eating the dinner she cooked, she asked you 'Do you like what I prepared for you, honey?'. Lying that the meal was good even though it wasn't increasing your chances of getting more cooked dinners in the future. Stating the truth outright might have changed the situation to an uncomfortable one. You lied because you'd benefit from it. And that's the main reason why we lie.

This is just one application and there are a lot of areas where some people might benefit through lying. A used car salesman trying to close a sale may deceive a potential buyer by giving inaccurate information or even skipping important data. There are even professions that may require people to lie like being a spy. When a person is accused and is facing a lot of time in jail, lying in order to walk away free becomes a huge incentive. Although moral issues may stop us from lying, anything goes when the stakes are high.

Since the development of language, humans have used or abused it to lie. To counteract this deception, social rules and rituals have been developed and members of these societies were required to adhere to these to become a member of the group. This gave birth to religion and along it came strict rules against lying and accompanying punishment for people who lied either in this life or the next (as some religions teach).

Language and rituals evolved together which led to today's sophisticated societies with complex norms and cultures on lying. As children, our parents told us not to lie but what they preach might not be consistent with their actions or behavior.

For example, a mother planning a surprise part for the father might tell the child not to tell him about the cake inside the fridge. That's basically telling the child to lie and this contradiction remains with us until adulthood.

The world is full of lies and liars and we also constantly think of lying when we think it suits us or it's appropriate to do. That's why everyone is interested in spotting non-verbal cues usually associated with deception. But can you really detect if someone is lying?

Body language researchers seem to be divided into two groups with regards to accuracy of detecting lies.

One group believes that specific gestures that can be associated with deception and if these gestures are observed in clusters, it's an infallible sign that the person is lying. This group is represented by Allan Pease who have listed, and categorized gestures associated with lying such scratching the neck, touching the nose, rubbing the eye, grabbing the ear, and so on.

The other group, led by Joe Navarro and is joined by Aldert Vrij, Matsumoto, and Paul Ekman, insists that non-verbal indicators can't be used to conclude that someone is lying. They believe that reading body signals such as grabbing the ear, etc., is futile because people who have become very good at lying already know how to avoid these gestures and will be able to deceive other people easily. These are people who gain the most benefit out of lying and are so careful not to get caught that they tend to overcompensate with their actions like gazing at you intensely instead of avoiding eye contact.

Common Lying Gestures

Most lying gestures are brought about by stress. The higher the level of stress, the more we instinctively display non-verbal cues. These nonverbal signals can be used to conclude that the person is under stress because he or she is lying. But keep in mind that the stressful situation itself might make the person show signs of stress and not because they are lying. Being accused of a crime or being arrested are examples of such stressful scenarios. When evaluating these lying gestures use the five Cs of body language.

Touching the nose. The person makes several rubs and touches on or just below the nose. When we think hard or are under stress, the body pumps more blood into our brain to help it perform the necessary computation or analysis and also help it to cool down. The increased blood in the head area dilates blood vessels in your nose which can then make it itch. We usually address this itch by scratching, thus this classic gesture. Again, consider everything before concluding that this is a sign of lying. A person scratching his nose may just have, well, an itchy nose!

Blinking rate. Stress can make a person blink more and faster. Within a given time, the more we blink, the more we are stressed. Normally, we blink five to six times in a minute. That's once every 10 to 12 seconds. When stressed, a person may blink five to six times in rapid succession. Dopamine production in the body affects the rate of our blinking and stress may induce its release into the body.

Touching the eyes. The person rubs his eyes using his finger. Fatigue is usually expressed by rubbing our eyes using a closed fist. Rubbing the eyes with a finger is suggesting that the person doesn't want to look into the outside world, maybe because he is lying. Due to feelings of shame, a liar may not want to see the face of the other person and rubbing the eyes with a finger accomplishes that.

Touching the mouth. The person places a finger or most of the hand on the mouth. Covering the mouth by touching it with a finger or with the whole hand might be an unconscious way to prevent the mouth from telling a lie. It's like physically stopping the words that are coming out of the mouth and this gesture is mostly observed on children. As we grow into adulthood the gesture becomes more subtle so we might just use a finger or two. Still, it's an indicator that a person might be saying things that shouldn't be said.

Touching the neck. The gesture might include one or more of the following actions: stretching the neck, fixing the tie, adjusting the collar, touching the dip in front of the neck, touching the sides or back of the neck, and touching the necklace. Covering or touching is usually associated with defensiveness and is commonly exhibited when a person is threatened. Like most nonverbal cues, touching the neck becomes most meaningful and expressive when the person is emotional. This gesture is also interpreted differently between genders. Women tend to touch the suprasternal notch or that dip in front of the neck or touch the side slightly. This can also be shown playing with a necklace. Men, on the other hand, tend to rub the front, sides, or back of the neck which has a calming effect because the action stimulates the carotid sinus and valgus nerves as an attempt to lower down stress levels. These gestures often suggest deception, insecurity, feeling threatened, and doubt.

Hiding a hand or both hands. The person hides his hands from view by putting them behind, placing them below the desk, or putting them inside pockets. When we can't see a person's hands, we instinctively become suspicious that he might be hiding something threatening. This makes us distrustful and uncomfortable. Again, this gesture should be taken in full context because it may not necessarily mean he is up to something. Look for other nonverbal signals while being aware or your unconscious reaction. Also, you shouldn't hide your hands when taking to other people if you want to gain their trust.

Excessive sweating. A person excessively sweats, and he hides it by pulling on his shirt to let air in, lifting or tilting his hat, or comb his hair a few times to cool down his head. Lying can be stressful to most and when we are stressed, we perspire more than the usual because we feel hotter. Sweat may then appear on a lying person's neck, cheeks, or forehead and he might try to hide it by cooling down using the mentioned gestures. But before you make a conclusion, consider other factors that may have brought about the excessive sweating such as the weather, the environment, and the other person's recent physical activity.

Tight or pursed lips. A person tightly presses his lips together. Compressing the lips is a common reaction when we feel threatened, worried, afraid, or just going through a negative emotion. Tightly held lips might suggest that the other person is stressed. You can then look for other nonverbal cues to see if that person is lying or trying to deceive you.

Eye contact. A person glances away or avoiding eye contact while talking to you. Eye contact is the most controversial gesture when it comes to pointing out deception. Generally, a person trying to avoid eye contact is lying although this may not be true in all cultures or nationalities. Latin-Americans and Africans, for example, avoid eye contact as a show of respect to authority. As previously mentioned, habitual liars have become so good at the lying game and some may go the other way and intensely gaze at you while speaking. Use gesture clusters instead to interpret the other person's intentions more clearly.

Talking rapidly. A person talks quickly and rapidly effectively preventing other people to talk. That person might be able to say a lot by talking rapidly but it can also distract and confuse the listeners. Often, the goal is to divert the attention from the main topic and move on to the next one. Sales people usually employ this technique as well as other who need to lie to make a living or survive. When you are bombarded with details, you tend to overlook other crucial factors and forget to ask important questions and eventually, you get deceived.

Delaying strategies. This nonverbal cue can be shown by talking slowly when required to answer crucial questions or creating distractions such as adjusting clothing, showing interest in something not related to the topic at hand, trying to shift the topic, or inviting someone else to join the conversation and change the topic. A liar takes time to think over the current situation and make the lie more convincing. To do this, he will use different nonverbal tricks to delay the answer to some questions or completely change the topic to escape interrogation.

Actions of a Liar

- Instead of relying on memory, they spend time thinking of answers

- They tend to touch part of their bodies which is a sign of anxiety or stress

- Try to avoid eye contact (because of guilt), or try to overcompensate by doing more eye contact than normal

- Observe you intently to see if you are buying into the deception

- To protect themselves, they may adopt a defensive gesture unconsciously

- Talk less to hide some details or talk a lot to confuse

- Keep repeating the questions asked in order to gain more time to think through their answers

- Tend to use long pauses in order to force you to talk and fill the gap

- Tend to avoid sensitive questions and try to change the topic of the conversation

Actions of a Truth-teller

- Tend to answer quickly from memory and facts

- At ease when talking about the topic and exhibit a comfortable and confident stance

- Talk at normal speed because there's no need to think hard

- Have an open posture and show their palms when talking

- Happy to talk about the topic as long as required

So, can you really spot a lie through body language? It all depends on how much you know the other person. If you know their behavioral pattern, their history, and consider all nonverbal cues along with the words spoken, you may be able to know if that person is lying or not. Otherwise, an extensive evaluation is required before you can conclude if the other person is trying to deceive you especially if they are good at it such as in the case of habitual liars.

Still, knowing these common lying gestures give you an upper hand when combined with other factors such as the person's character, verbal statements, and the other nonverbal signals taken into context. The goal is to check for emotional leakage or the unconscious exhibit of emotions which become clearer when the deceiver is going through a lot of stress.

# Chapter 9 - Body Language in Different Cultures

'There's language in her eye, her cheek, her lip.'
– Troilus and Cressida, William Shakespeare

A large part of the nonverbal communication among humans is made up of body language. We use facial expression, gestures, and eye contact to convey meaningful messages without the need to utter a single word.

However, how body language is used by people can differ substantially between cultures. Most of the times, the differences can be very subtle but sometimes, it's pretty obvious.

When visiting emerging markets or working in a company with a diverse culture, interpreting the meanings behind other people's body language may prove to be quite a challenge.

The Handshake

The handshake seems to be a universal gesture of greeting. That's because of the widespread western culture. But even this simple gesture can vary from one culture to another.

The firmness expected from a handshake may vary depending on location. A strong, firm handshake is perceived by Westerners as implying confidence, authority, or warmth. In most of the Far East, however, a strong handshake might be taken a sign of aggression. Bowing is a more accepted greeting gesture.

Even Western cultures may have differences in the length of handshakes. A firm, quick handshake is the norm in some parts of Northern Europe while in Southern Europe, handshakes are warmer and longer and both parties usually touch the clasped hands.

In some African countries, a loose handshake is considered the standard. In Turkey, a firm handshake is perceived as rude. In Islamic countries, men don't shake hands with women that are outside the family circle.

Hand Gestures

To 'illustrate' what we are trying to say or to emphasize points in our discussion, we often use hand gestures. But hand gestures can mean very differently between nationalities and cultures.

The universally accepted 'OK' sign where you form a circle with your thumb and index finger and lay out the rest means you're calling a person an a**hole in Brazil, Spain, or Turkey. This gesture is an insult to gay people in Turkey while in Germany and France this signal 'nothing' or 'zero' and is a sign for money in Japan particularly in a professional setting. Be careful using this gesture in some Latin

American, Arabic, and Mediterranean cultures because it's an obscenity for them.

The thumbs up, another common hand gesture which implies approval in European and American cultures means 'up yours' in Middle Eastern and Greek cultures.

The gesture that you make when you're beckoning someone by curling your index finger with palm facing up is accepted in Europe and America, but it's considered rude in some Asian countries such Singapore, Malaysia, and China. The gesture is usually only used to beckon dogs in most Asian countries and in some of these cultures, you can even get arrested.

In most Latin and Mediterranean cultures such Portugal, Italy, Spain, Cuba, Colombia, Brazil, and Argentina, raising the fist with the little and index finger extended is a way to tell people that their being cheated on by their spouse. That's why people in these parts of the world were astonished when President George W. Bush made the gesture during Inauguration Day in 2005 although he was just imitating the logo of the Texas Longhorn football team.

Facial Expressions

In a study made by the Paul Ekman Group, they created more than 10,000 facial expressions and presented them to different cultures, both civilized and isolated. They found out that people from these diverse cultures recognized more than 90% of the common facial expressions. Most facial expressions are considered universal.

There are seven facial expressions that correspond to particular facial emotions.

Happiness – Mouth corners raised, muscles around eyes tightened, and cheeks raised.

Sadness – Mouth corners lowered; inner portion of brows raised.

Surprise – Eyebrows arched, mouth open, sclera exposed, eyelids pulled up.

Fear – Eyes opened wide, brows arched, mouth opened slightly.

Anger – Eyes bulged, inner brows pressed together, lips firmly pressed.

Disgust – Upper lip raised, cheeks raised, nose wrinkled, brows lowered.

Eye Contact

Eye contact is an indication of attentiveness and confidence in most Western countries. When someone we are talking to is always looking away, it may mean that they're uninterested and looking for other people to talk to.

Eye contact between same gender in most Middle Eastern cultures are more intense and sustained compared to how Western cultures do it. In some countries, eye contacts that linger more than a brief glance are considered inappropriate and unethical.

Such as the case in many Latin American, African, and Asian countries wherein sustained eye contact is considered confrontational and aggressive. These people are very hierarchy-conscious, and they see avoiding eye contact as a sign of respect for elders and bosses. In these countries, children are taught not to stare at adults speaking to them and the same goes between employees and bosses.

People in Japan and Finland can get embarrassed when people are staring at them and eye contact is used only in the start of the conversation.

Here's how eye contact vary by culture:

- Should be used with care in most Far East nations

- Should be used with limitations in cultures including Thailand, Korea, Middle East, and Africa

- Often used in much of North America and Northern Europe

- Very common in regions including Latin America, Europe, and Middle Eastern and Mediterranean cultures.

Head Movement

As a gesture of confirmation or to show attentiveness, people in some parts of India tilt their heads from side to side. This head movement can be traced back to the British occupation of the country wherein in Indian people were scared of gesturing negatively to British soldiers, but they wanted to show that they understand.

In Japan, nodding means that you heard someone's statement but doesn't conclude that you agree.

Touching the Nose and Ears

In most Western Cultures, it is perfectly fine for people to blow the nose into a napkin or handkerchief. The same action, however, is considered dirty and very rude when done in front of a Japanese.

When Italians tap their nose when conversing, it often means 'watch out'. In UK, the same gesture means the topic is confidential.

Tugging the ears in Portuguese cultures means the food is delicious. In Italy, this gesture can have sexual connotations and when Spaniards do it, it's a signal that someone isn't paying for the drinks.

## Kissing and Using the Lips

When Americans need to point toward something, they use their fingers. Filipinos, however, often use their lips and might be perceived as offering a kiss.

Kissing in public in some European cultures to say goodbye or hello to a love one is considered normal. These gestures imply intimacy in Asian cultures and only done in the privacy of the house.

## Touching

Far East and Northern Europe are considered non-touch cultures. Beyond the normally accepted handshake, physical contact is minimized with people that they don't know well. An apology is expected when you brush someone's arm even though it was accidental.

Michelle Obama, US First Lady made headlines in 2009 when she broke royal protocol by hugging Queen Elizabeth. Something that is not usually seen anyone doing to the monarch other than family members.

In the cultures of southern Europe, Latin America, and Middle East, however, physical touch is an essential factor in socializing. In many Arab countries, for example, men would kiss each other and hold hands in greeting although they don't the same with women.

In South Korea, older people can touch the younger ones when getting through the crowd but it doesn't work the other way around. In Thailand and Laos, it's disrespectful to touch someone's head, even a child.

Here's how physical contact vary by culture:

- Low contact cultures avoid physical contact in general and people allow distance when talking. This is a practice seen in much of the Far East.

- Medium contact cultures touch on occasion and people stand quite close to each other. These cultures include North America and Northern Europe

- In high contact cultures, physical contact can be seen more often and people tend to stand close. Examples of these cultures are Middle Eastern nations, Southern Europe, and Latin America.

Touching rules are often very complex and might differ depending on the status, profession, ethnicity, gender, and age of the persons involved.

## Sitting

When dining or attending meetings with people of a different cultures, you should always be conscious of your posture. In Japan, for example, sitting with your legs crossed implies lack of respect especially when done in front of someone more respected or older than you.

You may offend people belonging to some parts of India and Middle East when you show the soles of your feet or shoes. President George W. Bush experienced this disrespect first-hand when someone threw a shoe on him while he was visiting Iraq in 2008.

## Silence

Silence is used in meaningful ways by some cultures. In China, being silent during a conversation implies receptiveness and is used to show agreement. In most aboriginal cultures, contemplative silence is expected before answering a question. Silence, when coming from Japanese women, is considered a show of femininity.

In most Western cultures, however, silence is seen as a negative action. The void in communication is seen as problematic by British and North American people. Silence is viewed as uncomfortable during interactions with friends, or in school or work. It often implies lack of interest or inattentiveness.

Gender

In most cultures, what is considered as acceptable for men may not be so for women. An obvious example will be covering the head in Muslim nations. Shaking the hand of a woman within religions of Hinduism and Islam is also considered offensive.

With increased expendable income and modern transportation, people are allowed, more than ever, to visit different cultures in the world. But before visiting a country, you must learn about its people's communication styles, values, and etiquette as much as you can. Physical contact, greetings, eye contact, and body gestures can have significantly different interpretations in different cultures and countries.

Understanding these cultural differences can help improve working relationship and can increase your chances of success in a world that is increasingly getting more multi-cultural and globalized.

# Chapter 10 - The Five C's of Non-Verbal Communication

For the early human ancestors, decisions made instantaneously based on subtle visual clues may mean life or death. First impressions today still bring about automatic responses, but these may or may not be accurate.

When you see someone with arms crossed, do you think they are just feeling defensive using their arms as a barrier? Or is it an act of superiority and dominance. Or maybe it's just a comfortable position for them?

Nonverbal signals help you form these quick impressions, and this is a basic survival instinct. But although this innate ability may come natural and automatic, not all first impressions are correct and accurate.

The human brain is hardwired in a way that it responds automatically to particular nonverbal cues and this is a result of millions of years of evolution. But our ancestors were exposed to challenges and threats that were much different from what we should go through every day.

These automatic responses should be filtered and analyzed because we now live in a society wherein nuances and restrictions add layers to what could have been simple personal interactions. For example, a workplace setting wherein corporate culture and policies adds to interaction complexities bringing about a different set of guidelines and restrictions for behavior.

In her book 'The Nonverbal Advantage: Secrets and Science of Body Language at Work, author Carol Kinsey Goman formulated five filters that you can use to sift through first impressions. These are culture, consistency, congruence, clusters, and context and are collectively called the five C's of nonverbal communication.

Culture

Cultural heritage influences nonverbal communication. When reading nonverbal cues, the amount of stress that the person is under should be considered. A high emotional level brings up gestures that are specific to certain cultures.

Understanding cultural differences can help you read body language more accurately. Let's take the simple gestures for 'yes' and 'no' for example. When you are agreeing to something you move your head up and down, otherwise you do it from side to side. This is a common set of gestures for many cultures. The Eskimos, however, do it the other way. And what a big misunderstanding it could have been if you read the gesture the wrong way.

Another obvious cultural difference is proximity when talking with another person. People stand closer to each other when talking in Middle Eastern countries and this is an accepted norm in their culture showing more intimacy and closeness. The westerners, however, respect other people's personal space and tend to leave a bigger space in between.

Cultures may not differ only between countries but in different regions of the same country as well. Let's take Japan, for example. In Tokyo, the nation's capital, it's common to see people half-running around as they try to reach the train or bus on time on their way to work. This contrasts the leisurely gait of people from the provinces of Japan.

Another factor that may change a person's body language is his or her profession. A person standing or sitting down with back straight may be seen as someone brimming with confidence while someone with slouched shoulders and hunched back as an introvert. Someone who trained in ballet dancing or with the military will have properly upright posture while those who spend their days in office work might always slouch. But their postures may not define their personality nor their nonverbal communication cues.

Understanding the culture that you are currently in while trying to interpret body language is critical as this can modify the signals significantly.

Consistency

The baseline of a person's behavior is when they are in a relaxed or stress-free condition. Understanding this baseline is important when trying to compare it with gestures brought about by stress or other stimuli.

Look at a person. How does he normally stand or sit when relaxed? How does he normally look around? When discussing a nonthreatening topic, how does he respond? This behavioral baseline can help you recognize significant changes in a person's gestures in different situations.

A teacher might have a student in the class holding up his head with the palm of his hand and quickly interpret it as boredom. But if the teacher looks for consistency, a pattern might show up that nullifies this first impression. So instead of blaming himself for the quality of his lecture, he can talk to the student on what makes him tired coming to the class.

This is a technique often used by police interrogators when checking for dishonesty on a suspect or a witness. He'll start with questions that are nonthreatening so he can make a baseline of the person's behavior when they are given no reason to tell lies. Then he'll start to bring increasingly difficult issues in the conversation and look for significant changes in body language that may indicate the person is telling a lie.

Basically, you need to examine whether the behavior being shown by the other person is atypical. If he's known to be someone who is habitually unflappable, warning signs should carry even more weight. Knowing that person's baseline behavior is very helpful before you try to interpret his expressions.

Congruence

When a person speaks and you can feel that the words, tone of voice, and body language are all telling the same thing, there's a good chance that you are getting a true signal. But when that person tells one thing, but the nonverbal signals don't show a similar pattern, you should be alerted that they're trying to deceive you.

This is called testing for congruence. When a person's thoughts and words are aligned which means they believe what they say, you'll see that their body language corroborate with what is being said.

If you are seeing telltale signs of incongruence, you may be able to conclude that the other person is not telling the truth. A person agreeing with what you said while moving his head from side to side or saying they're happy with slouched shoulders and head bowed down are examples of incongruence.

Supposed you had an argument with your partner and when you approached her after an hour to ask if she's still mad at you she answered 'NO!' with a stern voice and crossed arms, what do you think the real answer is? You can be pretty sure that she meant otherwise because her verbal answer is not in congruence with her body language.

Incongruence may not be a sign of an intentional lie and the person may just be undergoing inner conflict on what they're saying versus while they're really think about the subject.

Congruence between body and verbal languages helps create stronger trust between two parties. It maybe from one person to another or an audience. When your verbal cues are aligned with your body language, you are perceived as being authentic and people will see that you are someone worthy of their trust.

Clusters

During a conversation, you might see dozens of different nonverbal signals from the other person. In situations like this, you should not be putting significant meaning on any single action. You should instead be looking for clusters.

A gesture cluster is a group of actions, postures, and movements that indicate a common point. A single gesture such as crossing arms can be interpreted with different meanings or it may not have any meaning at all. But when combined with other nonverbal signals like a stern look, a headshake, or a scowl, the meaning becomes clearer.

That's why you should always be looking for behavioral clusters. A single gesture when viewed independently might have a different meaning when combined with other nonverbal signals.

A sad face may or may not indicate anxiety but if you see other indications, the symptoms begin to become clearer. Other signs may include foot movement, shifting of weight, heavy swallowing, rapid blinking, heavy perspiration, and rubbing of palms seen from the other person indicate an anxiety attack. Something that is hard to conclude if you only focus on a single action.

Effective leadership, for example, requires you to level with your team members. During a staff meeting, you may take off your jacket and sit at the center instead of the head of the table might indicate informality to make others around you feel more relaxed. But it can be further emphasized by leaning forward when someone speaks, making eye contact, and showing interest on the subject. This is an effective way to conduct a meeting where there is an open exchange of questions and ideas without considering position or rank.

Context

Context is about considering everything going on around the nonverbal cues such as location, what previously transpired, anything else going on, and other factors that may affect the body language. The meaning behind nonverbal communication can significantly change when the context also changes.

Let's take crossing arms as an example. When a person is being scolded at and he crosses his arms, that can mean that he's being defensive and is preparing a reply. But when the other person is the one crossing his arms, it can mean a show of superiority or authority.

Location also has a significant effect on the meaning behind body language. A person shivering slightly and hunching over while waiting at the bus station might be thinking 'it's really cold out here!'. While another person doing the same actions but sitting alone inside a comfortable office might be thinking 'I need help!'.

When you think of a man flailing his arms and screaming loud, you might immediately interpret it as a reaction to danger. But when another man is doing the same action during a football game, your perception of his behavior changes.

When you're having an informal talk with a friend and he touches his nose, that usually means nothing or just an itchy nose. But if that same friend is on a witness stand and has not touched his nose for an hour but did so when asked with an intimidating question that could indicate deception. The context changed your perception of his body language.

The relationship between two people can also significantly affect the context. When you talk with your team member, boss, or customer, you might display different nonverbal signals depending on who you are communicating with. Other factors that you may need to consider are past encounters, time of day, and the setting of the conversation (public or private).

# Chapter 11 - The Art of Seduction through Body Language

The act of attracting a mate is innate amongst all animals, humans included. We often see documentaries of male birds doing courting dances to gain the attention of the female and earn the right to mate with her. Other animals vie for attention through physical means wherein the winner becomes the father of the future offspring of the pack.

Drawing Attention

Have you ever seen a scene from the movies wherein a lady drops a handkerchief on the floor and then she bends down to pick it up which draws the attention of males? That's a classic seduction move. You can even try it yourself. Drop a napkin, a watch, a book, or a glove then pick it up.

We are programmed to notice actions or movement so other people will notice you when do this move and you draw attention to yourself. Getting the attention of a potential partner is an ice breaker and a great first move.

Appearing Vulnerable

For females, this is done by showing the back of the wrist or tilting the neck and exposing it. For both sexes, it can be done by wearing an open collared shirt and then touching the collarbone or the neck itself.

So how does this action work in seducing the other sex? Well, the back of the wrist and the neck are considered vulnerable body parts. When you show these parts uncovered or undefended to another person, it's an indication that you do not fear them, and you are putting your trust in them. This vulnerable body language might also imply that you are willing to entrust other vulnerable parts of your body.

Mirroring

This move is done by mirroring or copying the actions of the target of your seduction. When that person crosses legs, you do the same. When she touches her neck, you copy it. When he brushes his hair with his hands, you do the same.

When you copy the other person's movements and move in synch with him, your body languages match with his. He will see it as an implication that your thoughts are the same. Unconsciously, the other person will recognize the nonverbal cue and during this encounter he'll begin to feel more and more comfortable with you. In general, we are naturally attracted to people who are like us not so much in physical appearance but more on thoughts and actions. Mirroring is an unconscious move which makes it a very effective seduction technique.

Being More Visible

Walk or stand closely to the object of your seduction. Make sure that you are within the field of that person's view and that you do it more often compared to others, so you stand out. Bumping into that person intentionally a few times will make you a familiar face. To break the ice, you can also start small conversations so that you become strangers no more.

If people see you often, it's likely that they'll become more and more interested in you. This familiarity will lead to interest. This is a method being used by politicians and people in showbusiness. Be around your target often and be so more than others. In time, your target will pay more attention to you.

As a practice, just say hi to someone you don't know and do it on several different occasions. Eventually, you will become a familiar face to this person. Familiarity makes it easier to interact with that person. You can then become friends and maybe take it a level higher after some time.

If you are not noticed by your target, you are not being seductive. The body language of seduction is always about attracting attention.

## Appearing Approachable

There are two women who are both equally physically attractive. One has her arms crossed and head held high. The other one has her head tilted down and looking at you with her eyes. Who do you find more approachable? Of course, it's the second lady.

Try to imagine a child looking up to a parent. This classic gesture is an imitation of that look. A child will always look up because of the height difference and with wide eyes. It's a gesture of innocence and it's often used by girls, consciously or not.

You can use the same gesture as an adult and imply submissiveness to your target indicating that you are welcoming and easy to approach.

## Touching

Touch your target's shoulder. Touch or hold his hand. Touching is a very effective seductive move that is also being exhibited by other animals.

When you are trying to seduce a person that you are still getting to know, an accidental touch can be a great catalyst. It can be a very light touch when you are sitting close to each other or when exchanging something. That touch will serve as an ice breaker and is a good starting point in seducing that person. This nonverbal signal technique works very well with people who come from cultures that are somewhat reluctant to touch.

The act of touching can be very powerful. One research showed that waitresses who touch their customers lightly when giving the bill receive larger tips than those who don't. The customers were not aware of the touch and just felt like giving a higher tip. This is a technique used by many waitresses. The touch actually registers unconsciously, and the recipients are completely unaware of the act.

Being Symmetrical

There is a correlation between sexual selection and symmetry as shown by research. We find symmetrical bodies and faces to be very attractive. This attraction to symmetry can be traced back to human evolution. Those unhealthy or unfit often have asymmetrical bodies and may be seen as unfit for reproduction. This is why people with symmetrical features are seen as more sexually attractive than those who don't

In a study made by Annika Paukner and Anthony Little on macaque monkeys, they found that these monkeys tend to look at symmetrical faces longer than they would nonsymmetrical ones. A symmetrical face can be perceived as an indicator of good health. Wearing clothes or makeup that will make you look more symmetrical can make you look more attractive to the other sex.

Being Eccentric

The appearance of being exotic or eccentric implies adventure. Change your look and surprise people by looking different from the boring and ordinary. A little fanfare or ceremony while presenting yourself can help create a lasting impression.

This technique was used by the master of seduction herself, Queen Cleopatra of Egypt.

In 48 B.C., Julius Caesar was having a meeting with his generals inside an Egyptian palace. A guard approached Caesar telling him that a merchant wanted to give him a valuable gift. When the merchant was allowed to enter, he was carrying a large carpet that was rolled up. When the carpet was rolled out, inside it was the young Queen Cleopatra half-naked. Caesar and everyone else was caught by surprise.

This act was carefully planned by the Queen and Caeasar found it so seductive that for 4 years, he was under Cleopatra's spell and charm. She continued the elaborate seductive game and completely captivated the Roman General.

First impressions last so you should plan your entrance well. Combined with an adventurous

look and seductive body language, you are
bound to be remembered by your target.

# Chapter 12 – How to Show Dominance through Body Language

People who want to imply being in charge usually use dominant nonverbal cues. These people may not be aware these body language signals may not even be aware that they are doing so and may just be a factor in their dominant personality.

Used properly, showing dominance though body language can help you gain respect and popularity, a method usually employed by politicians during the campaign period. Here are some actions that express dominance.

Appearing Larger

Appearing larger and more powerful is an important factor in showing dominance and this can be traced back to man's prehistoric roots. This action is also very evident in animals where in fights for dominance are often settled by size comparison, saving the parties involved from altercations.

This behavioral bias was inherited by modern humans and can be seen practiced when competing with others. Using the same size and body language signal, they try to show their superiority by appearing to be threatening and should be avoided. Here are examples of these size signals:

- Make your body appear bigger. A bigger person is often seen as more dominant and more threatening. If you have the height advantage, then good for you because you are already large, and this effect comes naturally to you. It's one of the main reasons why taller people tend to be more successful than others not only in sports but also in the corporate world. For the smaller ones, here are some gestures, postures, and body language tricks to appear bigger.

  o Place your hand on your hips. This will make you appear wider than you usually are thus adding to your size.

  o Stand upright. Straightening your back can add inches to your height.

  o Sit or stand with your legs apart. This is applicable to men and like placing your hands on your hips, it also adds to your 'width'.

  o Hold your head and chin up. Another technique you can use to add to your height.

- Stand higher. When you are standing higher than the other person, you are in a more dominant position giving you a natural advantage. You can do this by:

    o Stand while the other party sits. This instantly gives you the height advantage.

    o Stand on a platform or step to give you extra height when compared with the other party

    o Stand tall and straight. Tiptoe if you must.

    o Wear a large hat or wear high hell shoes

    o Style your hair to make you look taller. This is a common practice with women.

Remember, people who make themselves appear larger or bigger aim to be more dominant, threatening, or powerful.

Claiming Territory

Humans are quite territorial, thanks to our ancestral origins and heritage. People shot a lot of territorial signals and you can use these to predict behavior. When trying to be more dominant, you can do the following nonverbal signals to claim territory:

- Claim a particular area in a conference room, exhibition center, meeting room, or office room and expect other people to comply with the rules you set for that area.

- Invade the personal space of the other person to imply dominance. You can even emphasize the act with a touch like lightly holding the arm or patting the person's back which indicates ownership. A study showed that show of affection may not always be the reason when a man touches a woman. Instead, it can be a show of dominance or ownership.

- Invade an area currently owned by the other person. You can sit at the edge of that person's table or on their chair which is a common gesture of dominance. This move is often used by power-tripping managers or bosses who invade other people's territory to show them who is in charge.

- Touch or hold the other person's possessions. When this gesture is done with a relaxed composure, this implies that you own what they own which is another indication of domination. You may pick the other person's favorite pen or phone or rearrange their desk. It's like saying 'what's yours is also mine and you can't do anything to stop me.'

- Walk in the center of the corridor so that other people stay out of your way. This is a claim to common territory which implies authority and dominance over others. The same can be observed from some drivers during heavy traffic wherein they don't let other drivers merge into their lane.

- When the meeting room has a long table, sit at one end. This position is usually reserved for someone with a superior role or power. Sitting here emphasizes your dominance over others.

- When talking with a group, position yourself at the center which forces others to pay attention to what you're discussing. Since your back will be vulnerable, ensure that persons you trust are behind you.

Signaling Superiority

There are various direct or indirect power cues that you can show if you want to appear dominant particularly in social contexts. You can either plan these signals or improvise when the need arises. These power signals can be a combination of verbal and nonverbal languages. Here are some of the techniques that you can use:

Show of dominance through wealth

- Wear expensive clothes, watch, jewelry, accessories, and makeup. Doing so makes you appear rich, powerful, and well-connected.

- Show off your possessions indirectly. This can be done by paying hefty bills in a relaxed manner, flashing the latest flagship mobile phone, or driving an expensive car.

Show of dominance through control

- Order a staff or team member to bring you something in front of another person. This implies that you are in charge of the area. For example, you can tell someone to bring you a cup of coffee, print a certain report immediately, or have them call another person and bring that person into the meeting room.

- Controlling and giving orders can also be combined with a display of wealth to emphasize importance. For example, call your secretary while in the presence of others and have her book you a business class flight, a five-star hotel with all the bells and whistles, and a chauffeured luxury car. Showing that you can get whatever you want indicates power and dominance and this is a move usually exhibited by top corporate executives to impress their customers.

## Controlling Time

No, you don't need a time machine for this technique. Similar with dominating other people's space, you can control their time as well by setting a pace for them to follow. You can use nonverbal cues to exert time pressure on other people. Here are some verbal and nonverbal techniques you can use:

Interrupt

- Interrupt a discussion by leaving early or arriving late

Hurry other people

- Set a fast pace for other people to follow

- Walk using wide strides. This implies you're determined a certain goal quickly and that you are confident with your actions. When you're walking with another person, walk a bit faster to set your own pace. This shows who's in charge and the slower person will be forced to also walk fast in order to keep up.

- Talk faster than the usual. This force other to also talk fast and give you control of their time.

Slow down other people

- When talking with another person interrupt him by asking for a concise and brief talk. This implies you value your time more than his. You can also use this technique when breaking a pace set by another person so you can change the discussion's focus. This may also be effective in counteracting the hurried pace of a dominant person.

Facial Expressions

To show dominance, it's important to extensively use facial expressions to show power and control. Here are some examples.

- Avoid eye contact. To suggest that someone is not important to you, you can simply avoid looking at them.

- Make prolonged eye contact. When you gaze at the other person intensely while proving a point, it implies that you stand by your word and you're not budging an inch. It also shows dominance, being uncooperative and unwilling, and being strong-minded.

- Make a neutral face. This can be very useful during negotiations because making this facial expression can be interpreted by the other person that you are unimpressed. When you hold this facial expression while another person is pitching his product or case enthusiastically, it can cause him to buckle or be unnerved. This is often exhibited during academic debates when a domain or subject expert such as a professor wants to show dominance by showing that he's not interested with the other person's ideas.

- Smile sparingly. People who want to show dominance smile less often than the submissive ones. Although there's a chance that some people might dislike you, smiling less often shows you mean business and you are in control.

Display Your Crotch (Applies Only to Men)

Of course, you need to have your pants on when you do this move or risk spending the night inside the jail. Stand with your feet shoulder width apart with both feet firmly planted on the ground. This is called standing crotch display and is a very masculine way of highlighting your genitals to show dominance or superiority. You can emphasize this move by 'adjusting' or lightly 'touching' the crotch area. You can also do this technique sitting down by opening your legs and knees.

It's very uncommon for women to show this gesture because it can be interpreted as an invitation to sexual intimacy although some may do so as a show of strength and equality with men.

Counteract Dominance

But what if another person in the room is showing dominance using the techniques mentioned above? You can derail their actions by utilizing these nonverbal strategies:

Return the gaze. If the other person looks you in the eye longer than what you consider normal, look back and return the gaze. Doing so might get you distracted by their piercing eyes but there's a way around that. Instead of looking directly into their eyes, imagine a triangle formed by the eyes and forehead then look at the center of that triangle.

Initiate first touch. Just before that person is about to touch you, touch him first. Or retaliate with your own touch when he touched you. This shows that you're not one to mess with or dominate.

Take it slow. When the dominant person is trying to rush you, breathe slowly, remain calm, and slow down the pace. This can imply that there's no need to hurry. Show that the slower pace you're trying to set is more ideal and be persistent about it. This applies to both walking and talking

Use humor. A dominant person always aims to take over conversations. Break that dominance telling a joke and take back control of the conversation. You can get a laugh by telling a joke or using nonverbal funny actions. You can use this break to shift the discussion back to your preferred topic.

Body language can be used to show dominance and influence the action of others. You can also use it to counteract dominance being imposed by others.

# Chapter 13 – Making a Great First Impression Using Body Language

First impressions last – it's a cliché and a fact. There are situations when you'll only be given one chance to make an impression and blowing it may mean you'll never get that chance again. It can be an interview for a job, a sales pitch to a potential customer, or simply impressing another person.

If you start with a good impression when you are introduced to someone, subsequent interactions with that person become a lot easier. Also, people you impress will want to know more about you or what you offer, and they'll start to make assumptions which are often positive. Will it be worth dealing with you? Can you be trusted? How can someone benefit in knowing you better?

Of course, it will take a longer interaction than the initial impression to answer these questions accurately but when you make a great impression, you've already laid a good foundation. It's natural for humans to assume and make rational assumptions based on first impressions.

So how do you make a great first impression? You can combine body language and nonverbal cues together with verbal communication to make a positive impression that lasts.

Remember that when you talk to people for the first time, it is very much like advertising yourself. You need to plan the execution before the encounter so that you have control of your appearance, what you should say, and how you can express yourself better using gestures. Nailing that first impression is critical especially in a world with so much competition and capturing another person's attention can be quite a challenge.

Be Prepared

When it's the first time you'll be meeting someone, whether for pleasure or for business, ensure that you look your best. You don't want to look hurried or unprepared like you forgot something.

When you look unprepared, the person you'll be meeting will think that you are not interested with the meeting or with them. The first meeting will be a bad start if you want to establish a longer relationship or connection with that person.

Being prepared for the meeting can improve that first impression by showing the other person that they are important to you.

Actually, first impressions are not about you but rather how other perceives you during your first encounter. So, it's basically about the other person. It's about making other people feel that you can be useful to their lives by improving certain aspects and fixing some problems for them. Otherwise, there's really no reason for the interaction.

These body language guidelines can help you plan for your first encounters:

- Dress properly. Dress according to the occasion but do so that the other person feels comfortable around you.

- Arrive on time. This will show the other person that you are eager about the meeting and that you value their time.

- Be confident and resourceful. When you appear in control, the other person will think that you are worth dealing with.

- Be open and relaxed. Make that first encounter a relaxing one and free of stress.

Visualize Mentally

Visualization is a technique used by a lot of successful salespeople. It's about visualizing the scene in your head and practicing how you should act and react.

Before your meeting, run the scenario in your mind. How will you enter the room? How will you greet them? How will you explain the

111

purpose of your meeting with them? You should pay attention to the appropriate body language as you visualize. What will your posture be and where will you stand? How would you speak and what tone will you use? Which hand gestures and facial expression should you use? Where would you place your hands or arms? Where and how would you sit? If you are meeting with several people, who should you focus more on? Are you wearing clean clothes and shoes? How do you look? Is your body language matched with the intended goal and message?

These are just some of the questions you may want to go through as you visualize yourself on how you want things to happen during that meeting.

Use Eye Contact

Eyes are the windows to the soul because they can say a lot about you. When you lack eye contact when interacting with other people, it can be interpreted as submissiveness, weakness, anxiety, or disinterest. Certainly not things you want them to remember as their first impression of you.

When you are approaching the other person, immediately establish eye contact and use facial expression to show your interest in the meeting and the person. When you show interest, you get it back in return, so you make a great first impression.

Deliver a Great Handshake

The handshake is the most common greeting during first interactions. This gesture is very much common in the corporate world. Mirroring the other person's handshake is a safe way to do this gesture. If they are pressing firmly, follow the lead and do the same. If they prefer a lighter handshake, just copy it. Mirroring is also an effective way in establishing rapport with other people and making them comfortable when they are around you.

Avoid these handshake types:

- Aggressive. Pressing too hard during a handshake is not a good way to leave a first impression. Although it's an implication that you are the one in charge, this type of handshake can lead to resentment. Other cultures even find firm and strong handshake offensive and degrading.

- Double handed. You can often see this type of handshake in politicians. You use two hands to enclose the other person's hand as you shake it. When done with a stranger, it might mean sudden interest which might alert the other person and go on guard. Another type of double handshake is when you tap the person's shoulder or arm when you shake his hand. Some people might take this as invasion of their personal space.

Here are some tips to remember when shaking hands:

- Be ready. If you have something in your right hand, hold it with the other hand, to prepare your right hand for the handshake. Remember not to put your hands inside your pocket when being introduced with other people. Some may take it as a gesture that you're not interested in shaking hands with them.

- Walk with confidence and firmly. A handshake often begins with an approach. Stand straight as you approach the other person, relax, and take your time being careful not appear too eager and hurried, but also not reluctant and too slow.

- Smile. To show interest, you should show a brief smile during the handshake. But don't overdo it because the other person might see it as a sign of manipulation and eagerness.

- Make eye contact. Remember to look the other person in the eye when making the handshake. To synchronize the act, a quick glance should be enough. Don't look at your hands during the handshake. The eye contact should last for only about three seconds. Be careful not to stare longer than 5 seconds when the other person is a woman. Anything longer may imply sexual interest which may not be your intention.

- Rise up. That is, of course, if you are seated and the other person approached you for the handshake. If you shake hands with them while remaining seated, it can be interpreted as a sign of indifference and that wouldn't be a good start. You may be exempted from rising up if you are eating, if you're a woman, and if it's acceptable to be seated when you shake hands with other people.

- Open your palm. Shaking hands with an open palm suggests honesty and being open to the other person. If you avoid touching palms, it may mean you are hiding something or be taken as a gesture of deception. That's why limp handshakes should always be avoided.

- Don't dominate. The best start to any relationship, be it for business, friendship, or romance, is to show that no one dominates, and both are equal. Ensure that the hand is straight, and the thumb is on top. The palm should not be facing slightly downwards or upwards.

Say Their Name

When meeting someone, mention their name two times during the first three minutes of the conversation. Your name is very familiar to you, perhaps even the most familiar sound in the world for you. You learn your name early in your life and may have been one of the first words you learned to speak.

When you say the other person's name make them feel interesting and important. Repeat their name to help you remember and also to imply being attentive and you care. Showing you care is an important part of establishing rapport.

Remember Their Name

If you keep on mentioning their name during the conversation, you impress them because you're making an effort to learn and remember their name when most people won't bother. This makes you stand out from the rest. Here are some techniques you can use to help remember a person's name:

- Remember the name. Make sure that you remember the name of the person the first time you hear it. This should be done with every people you meet. If you don't make an effort to remember the name, you are most likely not to mention it during the conversation.

- Learn the name. You may ask how the name is pronounced or spelled to make sure that you are saying it right. If you are doubtful about pronouncing the name correctly, there's a good chance you won't be mentioning it. It will also be awkward to ask for their name again so get it right the first time. Spend time learning the name when they say it so you can pronounce it correctly. Showing interest means you care.

- Repeat the name. As previously suggested, mention the other person's name two times during the first three minutes of the conversation. But don't overdo it or you might sound like a desperate salesperson.

- Lock the name in your memory. A very good technique in remembering names is to associate them with things or familiar sounds. This makes it easier to remember the other person's name.

- Write down the name. After the conversation, you can also write down the name of the other person together with a quick list of important points during the encounter and how the person strikes you. Don't be too

117

confident that you'll remember it in your head. Use your smartphone and jot down notes along with the person's phone number if they gave it to you. Or go old school and write it on a piece of paper.

Don't Fidget

Fidgeting gestures such as playing with your hair can be interpreted as sign of uneasiness and stress so they should be avoided. When you fidget, the other person can also get distracted by your actions.

# Chapter 14 – Improving Personal Impact through Body Language

Your personal impact is how people remember you, respect you, and listen to you. People with strong personal impact possess presence wherever they are. They are often perceived as successful because they always know what they want and always seem confident in any situation.

One of the goals you should aim for is standing out from the competition but in a good way and improving personal impact can help you attain it. With a strong personal impact, you leave a positive impression and people take you seriously. People also want you around and they interact with you positively.

One effective way of exhibiting positive presence is by using body language effectively. Think of any person that you feel has a strong charisma such as a successful businessman or a leader of a nation. Just the way they sit, walk, talk with others or just stand for a photo shows the powerful, influential, and important. That's because their body language is expressing their strong personal impact.

Here are some do's and don'ts to keep in mind when you want to have a strong personal impact.

Do's:

Mirroring

When you show you care, you build rapport and mirroring is an effective way to show this. Start by matching the way the other person talks by synching with the speed of talking and the tone of the voice.

Mirror the mood, facial expression, gestures, general posture, arm placement, and the sitting position. When you mirror their moves, it makes them feel comfortable when around you.

You can emphasize these non-verbal cues of mirroring by verbal mirroring using empathy. Basically, you just reflect on and repeat what they say. Mirroring can indicate that you are likable and trustworthy.

Resting Your Arms on the Armrest

When you sit on a chair with your arms placed on the armrest, you imply control and power. It's a very effective posture to take during meetings because it indicates you are relaxed and in charge.

It also makes other people more comfortable. In contrast, when you place your arms inside the armrest and towards your lower torso, it leads to a posture that may indicate defeat, fear, and weakness.

Controlling Emotional Bias

When you look at a picture of a person smiling, how do you react? You also tend to smile, right. You may not smile physically but you feel better inside. How about when the person in the picture is angry or sad? You mimic the emotions, too, right?

This is called emotional bias. Studies show that humans are hardwired to feel or mimic emotions by looking at specific facial expressions.

So how is it related to personal impact? People you talk to will pick up the emotion that you show in your face. They will then mimic that emotion and smile with you if you are smiling. This creates a positive feedback loop.

When you control the emotion of your audience, you have power. To make a person or group feel a particular emotion, you just initiate that feeling yourself. Your audience will then mirror that emotion and will actually feel it themselves. When you smile, your audience will smile back, which will make you smile even more creating an emotion loop. When you show a concerned face, your audience will also look concerned. This loop of negative emotion can make the atmosphere quite uncomfortable for all parties. You can see how this could have been avoided by flashing a simple smile. Even a face with a neutral expression can help calm another person. This way, you can increase your chances of establishing rapport before progressing to solving problems and addressing issues.

This method of using non-verbal emotional bias is also applicable when you want to influence the reaction of a group on something that they're experiencing for the first time. When there is a lack of a strong positive or negative feeling, the body language and overall mood tend to imitate the first reaction by any person in a group.

Suppose a salesperson is showing a new printer system to your team. Initially, there will be a show of neutral emotion by the group. If a member feels excited and enthusiastic about the product and he or she is the first person in the team to show this emotion, the whole group tend to follow suit and be excited as well. But if that person is unimpressed and looks bored, this negative mood will be followed by the group, too. So, in order to influence the reaction of the group, you should be the first person to express that emotion that you want to project to the group. Your reaction should be a combination of both verbal and non-verbal signals to double the impact.

Adopting a Positive Posture

As previously discussed, a posture can imply a particular emotion. So if you want to project confidence, you can simply raise your sternum which is the bone located in middle of the chest. You ever noticed that when you are feeling confident and energetic this bone shifts slightly upwards and outwards? This behavior is also shown by animals such as apes. When you do this intentionally, you tend to feel and appear confident.

In a research made in 2009 on posture's effect on confidence, test subjects were instructed to list their worst and best qualities. They were divided into two groups doing two different postures. The first was a confident posture where the chest was out and the back was straight. The other was a doubtful posture where they were slouching forward with the back curved. Test subjects who did the confident posture implied more confidence on both their positive and negative attitudes. The confident posture might not make a person feel more positive about the future, but it can them feel more confident on things they think about or do.

The confident posture is used commonly by politicians, public speakers, and professional actors to make themselves appear confident when in front of their audience. It might be a simple non-verbal signal, but you can achieve great results with it. Before entering a meeting or facing an audience, raise the sternum slightly, hold the chin high, take a few deep breaths, look ahead, smile, and proceed.

Lower Your Hands

Bringing up your arms while talking can be distracting to the other person. This can be interpreted as a barrier making your look defensive. You need to make careful gestures while expressing your statements and emphasizing the points you are making.

When you are talking to another person while standing, you may be holding a drink or something else in your hands. While conversing, you may use this object unconsciously like a barrier. This defensive position can come with negative consequences. If you're holding an object in your hand, just lower it while talking. If you are holding a notepad, don't place it in your front or hug it because it also acts as a barrier between you and the other person.

This also applies when you're holding a pen and you are moving your hand around while you talk which can be very distracting. To avoid scenarios like these, you should not be holding anything as much as possible. Remember that open palms imply openness and can make other people trust you more.

Looking from Eye to Eye

When maintaining eye contact, we tend to look at just one eye of the other person. Instead, you should look from one eye to another while you listen intently. Soften the expression you are trying to project with your eyes to imply that you care about their concerns and feelings. John F. Kennedy used this technique effectively when he talked to people.

Listening with the Body

We all want to know that we are being heard when we're talking. Everybody loves a good listener so if you want to improve your personal impact, you should strive how to be one. Here are some body language tips on how to listen while improving personal impact.

Leaning forward. When you lean forward, it suggests that you are fully attentive of the other person and that you are making an effort to hear everything that is being said.

Ignoring distractions. There can be a lot of distractions while you are talking with another person. Somebody dropping something, someone you know passing by, or a loud sound. If you want the other person to think that you are focused on the conversation, you should ignore all of these distractions. Maintain the current posture by controlling your body language instead of showing interest in the distraction. Ignoring these distractions is like sending a signal that you are very interested in them that nothing else can take away your attention.

Tilting the head sideways. Curiosity can be implied by tilting your head sideways. When you show curiosity, it means you are very interested in the topic or the person.

Nodding. This is another effective gesture of approval which you can use to gain the trust of the other person. When someone is explaining something, nodding will show that you understand or you're following what is being said. When you are talking to another person or a group and your audience remains still, you start to think that they are not actually listening to your or just daydreaming, so you naturally pause and ask them if they are able to follow.

Showing interest through noises. Your nod should be accompanied with verbal gestures that imply interest such 'wow', 'I see', 'Hmm', 'Uh-fa', and others to emphasize that you understand and that you are interested.

Adopting a patient posture. Showing patience is important when someone else is talking. When you glance at your watch, shift your weight from a leg to another, move constantly, or lean against a wall, it might be suggesting that you are tired, bored, or just want the conversation to end. You should instead show patience and focus through your posture and gestures. Avoid classic boredom signs such drumming fingers on the table or swinging your feet.

Don'ts:

Crossing Your Arms

Crossing the arms suggests defensiveness. Your arms can be seen as a barrier raised between the other person and you, indicating that you are raising your arms to protect yourself from them.

Research shows that we are more critical when the person we are talking to have their arms crossed. There is also less recall on the content of the conversation when a person has his or her arms crossed during the conversation. So if you want to be remembered or persuade people, you should avoid crossing your arms.

Touch Your Face When Being Questioned

Under stress, there is an increase in blood pressure in the facial area which may lead to itching in some parts, particularly inside the nose. Stress can also cause sweating on the neck or forehead which can also cause itchiness.

When this happens to you, you will be tempted to scratch. This may imply that you are lying or may not be telling the entire truth. Various body language books and articles have been written about touching or scratching as a sure-fire way to tell that someone is lying. Although this act may not really mean you are lying, it's better to avoid it can easily be misinterpreted.

This may require a bit of practice because it's easy to get stressed when you are being scrutinized. You can try reducing your stress levels or lessen the non-verbal cues that you give away when stressed. The first method is more effective, but achieving it needs more skill. The second one is doable, but it can be difficult to hide some non-verbal cues.

Reducing your stress levels means you need to remain calm in stressful scenarios. Regulate your heartbeat by taking slow, deep breaths. When you do this correctly, the stress will be significantly reduced, your nose won't be itchy, and you don't need to scratch it.

Rubbing the Back of the Head

When you rub the back of your head, it may suggest boredom or that you're just not interested. This body language can also suggest that you're thinking of leaving so you need to avoid it.

Keeping the Hands in the Pocket

128

When you put your hands inside your pocket, it may show that you are lacking confidence, or you are feeling insecure. Hiding the hands can also be interpreted as deception because it looks like you are hiding something. This rule also applies during public presentations. Putting your hands inside your pocket can be unconsciously interpreted that you are not confident with your claims.

# Chapter 15 – How Body Language Impacts Leadership

Being an effect leader requires an ability to positively impact and inspire people. When you prepare for a meeting with your clients, leadership team, or staff, you focus on what you would say, take note of crucial points, and practice the presentation so that your audience see you someone convincing and credible. These are things that you may already know.

But not everyone knows that when we talk to other people that we hope to influence, we are also being evaluated for trustworthiness, empathy, confidence, and credibility by our audience. And this evaluation is not fully determined by what we say. Gestures such use of eye contact, facial expressions, posture, and use of personal space can support, enhance, sabotage, or weaken the impact you are trying to instill as a leader.

Here are essential things that a leader needs to understand about body language and how it can impact leadership in general.

You Need Less Than Seven Seconds to Make an Impression

As previously discussed, first impressions are critical and this particularly crucial in business interactions. Once another person has mentally labeled you as submissive or controlling, suspicious or trustworthy, you will always be viewed through that filter no matter what you do. That means if that person likes you, they'll be focused on your best characteristics. But if you are labeled as suspicious, everything you do will go under the magnifying lens.

Our brain is hardwired to make snap decisions and this includes taking notes of first impressions. It's a survival mechanism and we can't do anything about it. What you can do, however, is to ensure those decisions are in your favor.

It takes less than seven seconds to make a first impression and this is heavily influenced by non-verbal cues. Actually, studies show that body language impacts your impression more than verbal language does by four times. So to make use of those valuable seven seconds, here are the things that you can do:

- Adjusting your attitude. People sense attitude automatically. Before stepping onstage for a presentation, entering the meeting room for a business meet, or greeting a client, assess the whole situation and consciously adjust your attitude to what you want others to see.

- Making eye contact. When you look at someone else's eyes, you transmit energy and indicate openness and interest. To improve this gesture, make a mental note of the eye color of every person you meet.

- Smiling. Smiling is very much underrated and unused by leaders considering it's a very positive body language. A smile is like a sign of inclusion and welcome – like an invitation. When you smile, you're saying 'I am friendly' without saying a word.

- Being mindful of your posture. A study made by the Kellogg School of Management at the Northwestern University showed that when you position yourself in such a way that you open up your body and take space, you activate a sense of authority that produce change in behavior of the people around you. This is called 'posture expansiveness' and it applies to all people independent of the role or rank in the organization. In many studies, posture has been found to matter more than hierarchy in the way a person thinks, acts, or is perceived.

- Leaning in slightly. When you lean slightly forward, it shows that you are interested and engaged. But you need to respect the personal space of the other person. In most situations, you should be around two feet away.

- Shaking hands. There is no quicker or more effective way to establish rapport than shaking hands. Studies show that a single handshake is equivalent to 3 hours (on average) of continuous interaction when developing the same rapport level. When you shake hands, ensure your palm fully touches the other person's. The grip should also be firm but not too tight.

You Need Verbal-Nonverbal Alignment to Build Trust

Your body language should be aligned with what you are saying in order to establish trust. If the nonverbal cues you are showing is not congruent to your spoken message, people will perceive internal conflict, uncertainty, or duplicity subconsciously.

Colgate University neuroscientists studied gesture effects using an electroencephalograph or EEG machine to measure brain waves that form valleys and peaks related to event related potentials. When subjects are shown specific gestures that contradicts spoken words, valleys appear. Interestingly, this same dip in the brain wave also appears when the subjects are made to listen to words that don't make sense.

This study shows that when a person says one thing, but the gesture is indicating another, it doesn't make sense to the brain of the recipient of the signals. When your words do not properly match your body language (declaring openness while crossing arms across the chest, talking about the stability of the company while fidgeting with the hands, conveying candor without eye contact), the content of the message is lost.

Talk with Your Hands

Whenever you watch a speaker who is passionate about the subject being discussed, you'll notice that their gestures are bigger or more animated. They move their arms and hands about to convey enthusiasm and emphasize points.

You may not yet be aware of this connection, but you have felt it instinctively. Studies show that an audience view people using a wider variety of gestures more favorably than those who don't. Also, people who communicate using active gestures are often evaluated as energetic, agreeable, and warm and those who don't move much are seen analytic, cold, logical, or mechanical.

This makes gestures an important tool in a leader's arsenal and proper use of them during a presentation helps create better and stronger connections with the audience. Even senior executives can make rookie mistakes when they don't use gestures properly. When they talk with their hands hanging limply on the side, people may think that there is no emotional investment involved or they don't believe the point that they are trying to make.

To effectively use gestures, you need to know how the movements are most likely perceived by your audience. Here are a few common hand gestures along with their meanings.

- Hiding your hands. Hiding your hands can make you look someone who shouldn't be trusted. This is a nonverbal cue that is ingrained deeply in the human subconscious. Our early ancestors had to make life or death decisions based on visual information coming from one another. When someone approaches without showing the hands, it can be taken as potential danger such as a hidden weapon. Although this threat is just symbolic nowadays, we still experience psychological discomfort when the other person is hiding his hands from you.

- Pointing fingers. This is a gesture often seen used by executives during interviews, negotiations, or meetings to show dominance or for emphasis. But this gesture is easy to overdo which might suggest that the leader has lost control making the scenario look like a parent scolding a child.

- Enthusiastic gestures. There should be a balance between energy and arms and hands movement. If the goal is to express more drive and enthusiasm, you need to increase the intensity of your gestures. But enthusiastic gesturing is quite easy to overdo and when it happens, it can be interpreted being less powerful, less believable, and erratic. An example of over-gesturing is raising your hands above your shoulders.

- Grounded gestures. If you want to make the audience think you're composed and centered, you should keep your arms within waist height and bent to around a 45-degree angle. Combine this gesture with a shoulder-width stance and you will appear focused, energized, and grounded.

## Face-to-face is the Most Powerful Communication Method

Video chats, teleconferences, texts, emails. Even in this tech-laden and fast-paced age face-to-face communication remains to be the most powerful, productive, and preferred method. There is no better medium to influence people than talking to them in person. In fact, the need for face-to-face interaction becomes more pressing for business leaders the more they communicate electronically.

So why are physical meetings necessary when you can chat with anyone in the world anytime you want? When we meet someone in person, the brain processes the stream of nonverbal signals which we then use as basis for building professional intimacy and trust. There is a lot of information that you can get only through face-to-face interaction. Spoken language is only part of the details we interpret when we talk with someone in person. We get most of the information facial expressions, pacing, vocal tone, other nonverbal cues, and the emotional clues hiding in the words. And to help us determine if the audience accepts our ideas, we look at their instantaneous response as immediate feedback.

This nonverbal link between people is so potent that we match our breathing rhythms, movements, gestures, and body positions subconsciously when we are genuinely establishing rapport with another person. A research showed that the human brain mimics not just the other person's behavior but the feelings and sensations as well during face-to-face encounters. Real communication can suffer, and our brains may struggle when pressed to rely on just spoken or printed word and denied from nonverbal cues.

There is no denying that technology is an excellent bridge for transporting information but if you're looking for positive client and employee relationships, the key is to meet them in person, face-to-face. This applies to all industries and across the globe because we all deal with people in our businesses. You may be tech-savvy but there's no replacing personal encounters when it comes to driving productive collaboration, engaging in fruitful conversations, and capturing participants' attention. That's why in some companies, employees are taught to send communication via email if it's not important, pick up the phone and call when it's important but not critical, and talk face-to-face when it's business critical.

Half the Conversation is in Body Language

More and more business executives are realizing the importance of body language in picking up and sending the right signals. When you are able to interpret nonverbal cues correctly and accurately, you are 'hearing' things that are not being said.

Communication has two main channels – verbal and nonverbal. That means when you are talking with someone in person, there are two conversations going on. Verbal communication is obviously important but keep in mind that not all content of the conversation is transmitted via spoken words.

If you're not able to read body language, you might be missing on important elements of the conversation that can impact your business either positively or negatively.

When launching a company initiative and you're sensing that the employees are not completely onboard, you need to determine what's happening and react quickly as a leader. You should be looking for engagement and disengagement signals from the people by monitoring their body language. Agreement, receptivity, and interest are indicated by engagement behaviors while defensiveness, anger, and boredom are all signs the people are disengaged with the idea.

Common engagement cues include nodding or tilting the head (a sign of giving the ear to someone) as well as open-body postures. People who are engaged should be facing you directly as if pointing to you using the body which is a clear sign of agreement. But when people are not sold to the conversation and they are feeling uncomfortable, they may slightly turn their body away from you at angle, which is a signal of giving a could shoulder. And if you can see them sit with legs and arms crossed, it's very unlikely that you'll get any cooperation.

Another way to check for engagement or disengagement is monitoring the amount or level of eye contact you get while talking to them. When we like some objects or people, we tend to look at them longer and more frequently. The average length of a normal eye contact lasts only around three seconds but when we agree with the other person, we look into their eyes significantly longer. The opposite thing happens when disengagement is apparent. We tend to take our eyes off people or things that bore or distress us. And this is what your audience might be feeling when you don't get enough eye contact from them.

As a leader, you should be body language savvy both in interpreting and implying the correct signals. Have you ever noticed how great leaders stand, sit, gesture, and walk in ways that shows status, competence, and confidence? When managing change and collaborative environments these leaders also send nonverbal cues signaling empathy and warmth.

Knowledge of body language can significantly impact leadership results because it can help leaders present ideas, bond with audiences, and motivate team members with increased credibility and a personal charisma style. A good leader should strive to develop these powerful skills and body language is the key.

# Chapter 16 – Improving Salesmanship through Body Language

As you are doing your sales pitch, a lot of thoughts run through your mind. What do you do to get their full attention? That guy is yawning. Is he bored? How can you ensure that you close this sale?

A great salesperson is aware of what their clients or customers truly feel which tells them how they should react. In short, you should become an expert in body language reading.

So why is body language a crucial skill in sales? When you interact with a prospective customer, you communicate on two levels – verbal and nonverbal. It's obvious that the verbal interchange but as previously discussed, words can be used true feelings or intentions. So in the midst of subtle personality complications and tricky negotiations, you can depend on your body language reading ability.

During your sales presentation, you should be actively monitoring your audience's informative nonverbal cues especially their engagement and disengagement behaviors. Engagement indicates agreement, receptivity, and interest on what you are presenting. Disengagement indicates disagreement, defensiveness, resistance, or worse, hostility.

These are behaviors that you can't get from verbal communication but are revealed by leg and feet movement, torso positions, hand and arm gestures, head movements, facial expressions, and eye activities.

You may think that it's impossible to keep track of these nonverbal cues while decoding complex verbal negotiation especially with a person you've never talked to before. In fact, you have been interpreting and reading body language signals and reacting to them all your life. The only difference in this scenario is that you should be mentally taking note of these cues, interpreting them to assess how the negotiation is progressing, and making required adjustments to increase the possibility of a positive outcome.

Here are some of those body language signals you should be watching for.

The Eyes

When you present your customer with a couple of different options, you may notice that the gaze lingers on one of the options longer than the other. That's an indication of interest on the first option which you can further exploit by elaborating on the benefits if the customer chooses that. This is further emphasized if the eyes are open wide and the pupils are dilated. You'll know that you've caught the customer's attention.

When people are drawn to objects or other people, they tend to gaze longer and more often. Even though a person pretends to be uninterested, his eyes will naturally keep looking back to that object or person he finds attractive.

It's also applies to eye contact. Studies show that if you want to create rapport, you should maintain eye contact with the other person 60 to 70 percent of the time you spend talking. In a negotiation scenario, people who agree with you or like you tend to look into your eyes longer.

On the contrary, if you are sensing low levels of eye contact, it can be sign of disengagement. When people are presented with objects or other people they don't like, they tend to look away. When your prospect is avoiding eye contact by looking around the room, defocusing, or looking past through you that may he feels restless and is bored. His eyes will also narrow slightly which is a signal for disengagement rather than opening wide. You may have observed people who are reading through proposals or contracts tend to narrow their eyes. This is a nonverbal cue which means he's seeing parts of the contract that he finds problematic or troubling.

It has been proven by many studies that our emotional responses affect the size of our pupils. And we practically have no control over our pupils. They just react to emotional stimuli, either external or internal. This fact makes pupil dilation an excellent indicator that a person is interested. There are a lot of reasons why our pupils dilate, and these include cognitive difficulty and memory load, but they also dilate as a way of expressing positive feeling towards another person or object. When a person is not particularly receptive, their pupils automatically constrict.

Facial Gestures

A nod and a smile coming from your audience when you speak is a clear indication of agreement with what you are talking about. Disagreement, on the other hand, is expressed by an awkward sideways eye contact, the head turned away slightly, clenched jaw muscles, tense mouth, lowered eyebrows, or pursed lips. Be aware of these facial gestures so you can adjust accordingly and gain their attention and interest back.

Hand and Arm Gestures

Take note of the customer's arms while he's talking to you during a sales pitch. The more open they are, the more receptive the customer is to the discussion. These should be welcoming, expansive gestures that flow naturally and do not look forced. By contrast, those who are angry or taking a defensive position may use their arms to 'protect' themselves by folding them across the chest, gripping the wrists or arms tightly, or clenching the fists.

During the negotiation process, you can depend on arm and hand movements to indicate subtle changes in your customer's emotions. At the start of the conversation, the customer's hands may rest on the table with the palms open. If they withdraw and place their hands under the table, it can be a cue that something unwanted or unsettling has happened which caused the abrupt change in emotion. A person who plans on making a sincere disclosure usually shows his hands by putting them on the table or makes open hand and arm gestures as they speak.

Torso and Shoulders

The torso and shoulders also play a critical role in body language. When your clients or customers agree with you, they tend to lean toward you or stand closely beside you. This is a sign of submission. But when they don't agree with what you're saying, they will try to stay at a distance from you or lean back in order to create additional space. These are gestures that are difficult to fake.

Also, when the customer turns his torso and shoulders away from your, there's a good chance you've lost his interest. Veering away from another person is a common gesture of

145

disengagement or detachment. It's as if the other person is trying to put up an invisible wall between the two of you. When your customer is engaged with the discussion, he'll face you directly by pointing at you using his torso. But when he feels uncomfortable, he'll turn away and give you a 'cold shoulder'. If your customer is being defensive, he may show it by an attempt to shield his torso with a laptop, briefcase, purse, etc.

When people are in agreement, they tend to mimic each other's emotions or behavior. One person leads while the other will follow. Notice the body orientation of your customer. Is it the same as yours? Try moving slightly. Did he mirror the movement as well? If he did, then you've definitely made a positive connection.

Legs and Feet

Our legs and feet are our primary means of movement. They are also great indicators of flight, fight, or freeze strategies for survival. These movement instincts are tied up to our DNA, so they respond before you even think about an action. The limbic brain system is responsible for this process and it's the one which makes sure that our legs and feet are prepared to run away, kick out, or just freeze in place, even before any conscious thought of what to do in a given scenario.

If you see that your customer is sitting with his legs stretched forward and ankles crossed, it can be a sign of a positive feeling toward you. But when his feet are pulled away, wrapped around a chair's legs, pointed to the exit, or in an ankle lock, this is a clear signal for disengagement and withdrawal.

Other legs and feet signals include:

- When your customer is bouncing his heels on the floor, it's an indicator of 'happy feet' which means he feels good regarding his bargaining position. If you are competing with another salesperson and you see him rocking back on his heels while raising his toes, he might be thinking that he's got the upper hand.

- When the customer's bouncing feet suddenly stops and go still, it may indicate heightened anticipation which is similar to holding your breath.

- Crossed legs are also good indicators of your customer's engagement or disengagement. When the leg on top of the crossed legs is pointed towards you, it's a sign of interest. When the top foot is pointed away, maybe towards the door, it's a sign of withdrawal.

When you are observing these nonverbal cues during sales negotiations, be vigilant but not too obvious. Just rely on your instinctive reactions but keep a mental note of all the body language signals. Remember that you have already been interpreting these signals subconsciously. The ability to read body language has helped our ancestors survived and it's been passed on to us. You just simply need to turn this instinct into an effective tool for success.

# Chapter 17 – Body Language Tips During a Job Interview

You might be wondering why you didn't get the job. You know that you nailed that job interview. You had the skills needed for the position as well as the experience. But still, you didn't get the job.

During that job interview, you might have said all the rights words. You answered everything asked of you to the best of your knowledge and you can see the interviewer was satisfied with your answers. But did your body language match up with the words?

In an interview made on hiring managers discussing reasons why applicants fail during the job interview, one of the reasons was that the interviewee neglected body language. As an applicant, the hiring managers look at the way you present yourself, the way you speak, and equally important, your body language.

You might be saying that you are open to new ideas, but you are sitting there with your legs and arms crossed which makes the interviewee question what's really going on inside your mind. To convince them that you have management skills, for example, you must carry yourself as a leader by dressing appropriately, speaking knowledgeably, and posing and gesturing confidently. Without all these factors, it will be hard to trust your assertion. Tiny details matter.

If your words are not aligned with your nonverbal signals (or vice versa) during the interview, there's a high probability you won't make it to the second interview or get the job offer. According to statistics, here are the following reasons why hiring managers didn't hire aspiring applicants and the percentage of how important these factors are:

- Not enough eye contact – 67 percent

- Lack of confidence and smile – 38 percent

- Bad posture – 33 percent

- Weak handshake – 26 percent

- Crossed arms – 21 percent

Imagined how the interview scenario would have changed if you knew these negative body signals and avoided them? Here are useful that will help you through your next job interview in flying colors.

Before Entering the Building

You may not know it, but the interview actually begins even before you're out of your car or the cab. You'll never know who's around watching you so you should start being aware of your body language as soon as you get out of the vehicle. If you look panicky or frantic, the right person (the hiring manager) who happens to be passing by in the parking lot might get the wrong first impression from you. So, before you get out of the car, take a couple of deep breaths to help you relax especially if you're feeling stressed or rushed. When you are already calm, grab that briefcase then get out with ease and confidence. Think like you already work there.

Maintain this confident image as you are entering the building. Even if you are worried of being a little late or nervous about the interview, keep your composure and don't draw attention to yourself. This way, you show that you are calm and prepared, just like what a professional should be.

While Waiting Patiently

Be courteous and respectful to the administrative assistant, receptionist, or the gatekeeper. As you walk through the office doors and approach the receptionist, continue with the same composure as when you got out of your car. Always be polite, and when told to take a seat while waiting, sit down facing the receptionist if possible. This is called the profile view. People feel more comfortable around you with a profile view so they're more likely to mention positive things about you when asked by the hiring manager. And hiring managers do ask their administrative assistants for opinions.

Keep your space clear and organized while you wait. Keep your lap clear of clutter by placing your purse or briefcase next to you. When there is clutter on your lap, it makes you appear unorganized and clumsy. It can even be awkward when you need to get up as you are called for the interview.

Don't be over-relaxed of overconfident. You can appear calm and confident but remember not to overdo it. Don't slouch or lean back too much or carry your head and chin too high. It might imply that you're overcompensating or just too bullish that you'll get the job easily.

Face the interviewer as he or she approaches. You can even do this before the interviewer comes out just find out where he or she will be coming from then face that direction. This allows for a graceful introduction as you get up and shake the interviewer's hand.

As the Interviewer Enters

Shake hands properly. The goal is for the handshake to be firm but not too strong that it seems like you want to break the interviewer's hand. But don't let it be too weak either as it's also a bad impression as much as a too strong one. To get it right, you can practice with a friend. Be sure that you use your right hand for the practice.

Ensure your hand is on the bottom during the shake. This indicates respect to the

152

interviewer's authority compared to yours. Also, you should not put your other hand on top while handshaking. This shows that you treat yourself as more superior.

Lead the interviewer lead the conversation while you follow. Remember your place. He or she is the interview and you are just the interviewee. You need to understand status and protocol and abide by them.

While Being Interviewed

Be open and not closed off. When you are seated, try not to lean forward too much as it may make you look closed off. The same applies to crossing your arms on your chest. To show that you are receptive, sit upright while your stomach, chest, and neck are showing. This posture implies that you're open.

Ensure that you have your hands above the waistline but below the collarbone. This is referred to as the 'truth plane' and it makes you appear more centered and calmer. Having your hands anywhere else make you appear nervous or frantic to the interviewer. When you gesture within the truth plane, you are perceived as someone who wants to help. And help is what the company needs. Else, they won't have a job opening.

Don't put up a barrier during the interview. Unless relevant to your interview, there should be no sheets of paper, folder, or anything on your lap or the table and between you and the interviewer. Else, it will seem like you are putting up a barrier and you will be seen as closed off.

Remember the power of eye contact. Avoiding eye contact seems to be the universal nonverbal signal of deception or lying so you should do it more often and longer during the interview. Whether you are speaking or listening, make proper eye contact.

As You Exit

When the interview has finished, make your exit graceful by gathering your belongings calmly and standing confidently. Make eye contact and shake hands with the interviewer with the same firmness as the one before the interview. If it's not too inconvenient or awkward, shake the hands of all the interviewers if there are more than one. Thank all of them while smiling and then exit the room gracefully and confidently.

The interview process continues until you get out of the parking lot. If it's not awkward, say goodbye politely to the administrative assistant or the security personnel as you leave the office and the building. Always think that somebody might be watching your move and you're trying to impress him or her. Wait until you are inside your car before making that exciting call bearing news of how the interview went.

Understand yourself better through body language because this will be helpful when you are called for a second interview. Be aware of how you are expressing yourself through nonverbal cues and you'll be more prepared the next time you are called for an interview.

# Chapter 18 – Showing Intention through Body Language

The way you position your body tells a lot about what you like or don't like. These nonverbal cues can show your true interests and intentions beyond spoken language. If you are consciously aware of these body signals, you can make changes to your posture to imply interest on something or somebody. You can also use it hide what's really going on inside your mind. To show intention, different parts of the body are utilized.

How You Orient Your Body

Generally, you can tell what or who a person is interested by the direction his or her body is facing. The mind leads while the body follows. When you are talking to someone and that person's torso is pointed away from you, this usually means that he or she is not receptive of your presence and planning to end the conversation by leaving. But when the torso is pointed towards you and the person is facing you directly, it implies interest, attraction, and the desire to continue talking with you.

Where Your Foot is Pointed

Similar to how the torso is oriented, when you point your foot towards somebody or

156

something, you are showing interest or attraction. In a group of people standing around while having conversations, you can quickly point out who amongst them is interested in someone else by interpreting their body language. If a person has his or her foot pointed towards you, he might be interested in striking a conversation with you. If someone has his or her foot pointed away from the group or towards the exit, it's an indication that they want to leave the group or join another group which they find more interesting.

Consider the following scenario:

- There are three persons having a conversation. Two males and one female. The female is in the middle. One of the males is on the right and the other on the left.

- The female's body and feet are pointed towards the male on the right while her head is facing the male on the left. She's also holding a purse placed on the left. This indicates that she is more interested in the man on the right although she might be conversing with the man on the left while the purse also acts as a barrier between them.

- The man on the left has his body and one foot pointed towards the male on the right which shows he is focused on the conversation with the other male. He also has his hands inside his pocket which can be a sign of lying deception. His other foot is pointed away from the group which may indicate an intention to finish the conversation and leave the group.

- The male on the right has his body and one foot pointed towards the male on the left. Similar to the other male, he's also focused on the conversation. His hands and palms are exposed which indicates openness and honesty. His other foot, however, is also pointed away from the group which means he also doesn't want to stay in the conversation.

When you consider the whole scenario, the female seems to be defensive, the male on the left is probably deceptive, both males are planning to leave, and there is no sign of agreement between the three persons.

How You Glance and Move Your Head

The same with foot and torso orientation, pointing the head towards an object or a person shows interest while pointing away suggests something else. This gesture is easier to notice so we are more familiar with it. We also often look at a person's head more than at their feet or torso.

Since the foot, torso, and head can move individually, we should read the overall gesture in clusters for a more accurate interpretation of the message behind the signals. The other person may glance around to see if other people are around and invite them to the conversation. Without considering the other gestures surrounding the scenario, you may interpret this wrongly as a loss of interest.

Displaying the Crotch While Pointing a Foot

This gesture applies to men only and is a variation of the standing crotch display but with the addition of a foot pointed towards the other person. This body language, when adopted by a man, often implies confidence and the desire to show that he is equal to or above the other person. It may also show interest.

Showing Inclusion or Exclusion of Other People

In a group of three people standing and conversing you can read their body orientation to know who are included in the group and who is being left out. If you notice two persons in the group are directly facing each other while the third person is isolated, this might indicate that they are not interested with that person and would rather want him to leave the group. Sometimes, it can be the whole body doing the gesture and, in some situations,, only the torso or the foot. That's why you need to learn how to interpret gestures in clusters.

How You Make Eye Contact

Eyes are said to be the most expressive part of the human body. This makes them an important part of the study of body language. To show intention or interest, eye contact is essential. You also get to look at the other person's eyes and be able to interpret hidden meanings behind their words.

It is a known fact that proper eye contact can help improve communication. Removing your sunglasses when talking with someone is critical if you want the conversation to be more personal and emotional. In a study, police officers removing their sunglasses when questioning other people get more cooperation than those who don't.

Showing interest or intention requires direct eye contact. Avoiding it usually implies shyness, disinterest, submissiveness, being trouble, or even potential deception.

Eye Movement

Eye movement can also be used to show intention or interest, or the lack of it. The positioning of the eyes during a conversation can tell a lot about what the other person is thinking. Various studies have been made around eye movement and its role in body language. One such mode is NLP. But like other gestures, you should interpret it only as part of a cluster. Here are the common eye movements or positions and their possible meanings:

Up and left – visual constructed images

Up and right – visual remembered images

Left – constructed sounds

Center – visualization

Right – remembered sounds

Down and left – kinesthetic, body sensations, touch

Down and right – auditory, internal dialogue

A more in-depth of the role of the eyes in body language is discussed in a chapter dedicated to oculesics.

# Chapter 19 - Influencing Your Emotions Using Body Language

You have learned that knowing how to read or interpret body language can help you better understand other people and making changes to your own nonverbal cues allows for the better communication. It turns out, however, that body language and the brain are in a two-way relationship. This means instead of your emotions influencing your body language, body language can influence emotions. Let's discuss some sample cases.

Smiling

It is a fact that when you are undergoing certain emotions like happiness, your body also undergoes biological changes which can make your heart beat faster, make you sweat more than usual, or move than involuntary muscle called the zygomatic major which makes you smile.

But did you know that it goes the other way around too? Changing the state of particular facial muscles like the zygomatic major by smiling consciously triggers the emotion that is associated with the expression, which in this case is joy and happiness.

This phenomenon is referred to as the facial feedback hypothesis. Charles Darwin, one of the greatest thinkers and scientists of the world, also suggested this phenomenon by indicating that physiological changes can impact emotions directly.

To test this hypothesis, a study was made in 1988 by Strack, et al. In this study, subjects were instructed to adopt a given expression but without the accompanying emotion. They were also not told what the experiment was all about to avoid bias.

In this ingenious study, the subjects were told the research was about determining how hard it is for people to hold something without using the hands. The subjects were divided into three groups.

The first group was instructed to hold their pens using their lips. This forced the expression of a frown.

The second group held the pen with their teeth. This forced the expression of a smile.

The third group served as the control and were instructed to simply hold their pens using their non-dominant hands.

All subjects rated the difficulty of holding the pen. For the real test, the subjects were shown a short cartoon film and were made to rate how funny the cartoon was. Those who held their pens using their teeth recorded the highest amusement rating amongst the three groups. This emphasizes the saying 'smile and the whole worlds smiles with you.' Smiling makes you happy and also make others happy. And when you see they are happy, you become even happier.

Anger

Another strong emotion but with a negative connotation is anger. Try this experiment. Make a facial expression that shows displeasure or anger by wrinkling or furrowing your eyebrows. This will engage the muscle called the corrugator supercilii.

How are you feeling while reading this sentence? When you make an angry facial expression, the brain gets the signals from the engaged muscles and concludes that because of the state of the muscle, you must be angry or upset. By adopting a certain physical state, like anger in this case, your emotional state was also affected.

A study even showed that when you make an angry face, you become more critical and harder to please. In one study, subjects were made to furrow their brows as they look at pictures of some famous personalities. The results of the experiment that when the subjects' brows are furrowed, they are less impressed by the celebrities and thought of them as not so famous.

In another study, instead of forcing the furrowed brows, an elastic bandage was placed on the foreheads of the test subjects artificially creating an angry facial expression without effort from the subjects. They were then made to rate neutral targets. And even though the furrowed brows were artificial, the facial expression still had the same effect on how the subjects judge things.

So, stop furrowing those brows and smile instead.

Confidence

In body language, confidence is often shown by a straight posture with the chest out, head held high, and the chin up. When you slouch, it may imply lack of self-esteem.

In another study, test subjects were divided into two groups and one was made sit straight while the other group was in a slumped posture. They were then made to fill up a job application form. In this form, they were asked to list their personal strengths and weaknesses related to the job. They were also asked if they consider themselves fit for the job using a rating system.

The experiment showed that those who took the slumped position felt less confident about themselves and also rated themselves less suited for the job. Again, this is a proof that how you carry yourself can have a significant effect on your inner thoughts and emotions.

# Conclusion

Body language is an exciting and important field. It can help you improve how you communicate with others because you will be able to interpret what others are really trying to say.

Using the correct body signals, you can show enthusiasm and attentiveness. You can also use them to influence other people's moods.

With the knowledge you have gained from this book, you'll be able to determine if someone you know is trying to deceive you. You can also go through personal or professional meetings with confidence.

The key is constant use and monitoring of body language. Looking for nonverbal cues should become second nature to you.

I hope you can put the lessons from this book into good use and get the results you desire.

Thank you.